Remembering
Lake Tahoe

Ellen Drewes

TURNER
PUBLISHING COMPANY

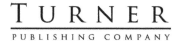

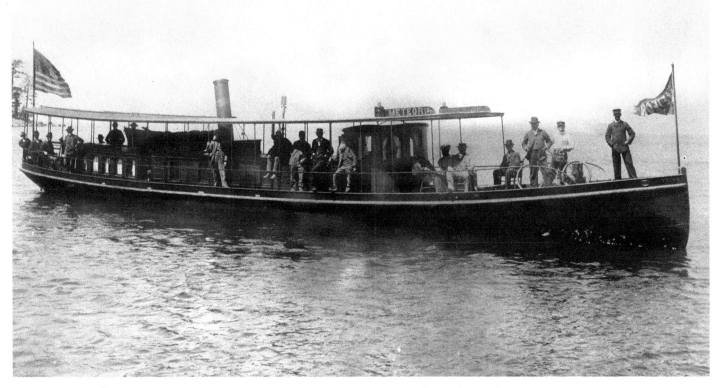

The steamer *Meteor* with passengers and crew visible. Launched August 27, 1876, from Glenbrook, the "Greyhound of the Lake" was at that time the largest and fastest inland waterway tug in the country, managing 20 knots and measuring 70 feet in length.

Remembering
Lake Tahoe

Turner Publishing Company
www.turnerpublishing.com

Remembering Lake Tahoe

Copyright © 2010 Turner Publishing Company

All rights reserved.
This book or any part thereof may not be reproduced or transmitted
in any form or by any means, electronic or mechanical, including
photocopying, recording, or by any information storage and retrieval
system, without permission in writing from the publisher.

Library of Congress Control Number: 2010932640

ISBN: 978-1-59652-714-0

Printed in the United States of America

ISBN: 978-1-68336-846-5 (pbk.)

CONTENTS

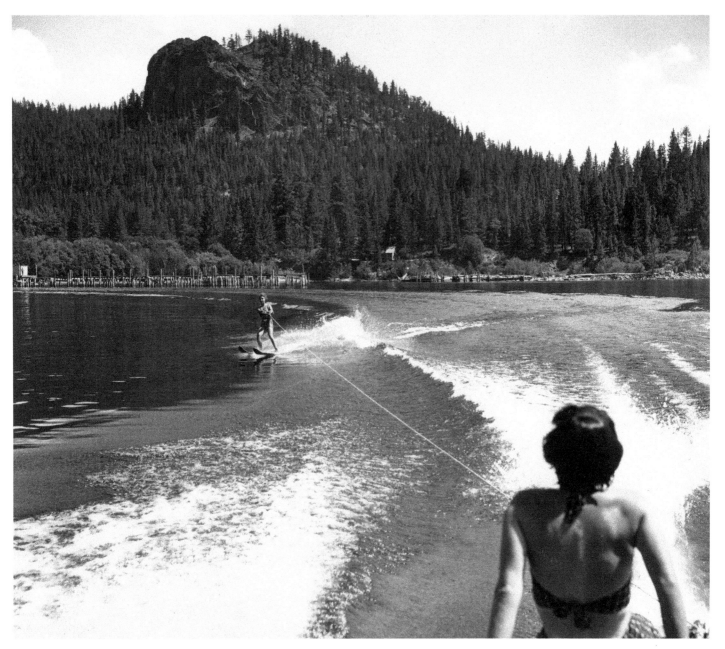

Water skiing on Lake Tahoe around the 1950s. From the boat, one woman watches as another skis the lake, with Shakespeare Rock in the background.

ACKNOWLEDGMENTS

This volume, *Remembering Lake Tahoe,* is the result of the cooperation and efforts of many individuals, organizations, and corporations. It is with great thanks that we acknowledge the valuable contribution of the following for their generous support:

Library of Congress
Special Collections, the University of Nevada, Reno Library

The author wishes to acknowledge Kathryn Totton, Photo Archivist in Special Collections at the University of Nevada, Reno Libraries, who has researched the background of many of the photographs in this book; Donnelyn Curtis, Head of Special Collections at the University of Nevada, Reno Libraries, who selected several of the photographs; Johanna Raymond and Melissa Rivera, student assistants in Special Collections who digitized the photographs; the many photographers who documented Lake Tahoe's history so beautifully, especially Gus Bundy; and the many donors who lovingly preserved and generously provided the photographs to Special Collections, especially Dr. James Herz and Bethel Van Tassel.

With the exception of touching up imperfections that have accrued with the passage of time, rendering color as black-and-white for a few of the later images, and cropping where necessary, no changes have been made to the photographs. The focus and clarity of many images is limited to the technology and the ability of the photographer at the time they were recorded.

PREFACE

"So singularly clear was the water that when it was only twenty or thirty feet deep the bottom was so perfectly distinct that the boat seemed floating in the air! . . . so strong was the sense of floating high aloft in mid-nothingness, that we called these boat excursions 'balloon voyages'" wrote Mark Twain. He was describing his idyllic encounter with Lake Tahoe, the largest alpine lake, one of the highest lakes, and the second deepest lake in the United States.

Crystal-clear Lake Tahoe is geographically unique, straddling California and Nevada and lying on a fault line that can subject it to earthquakes, and potentially tsunamis. Its history began with early inhabitants the Washoe, who made a summer pilgrimage from the Carson Valley to its cooler climes, and continued with explorers John Fremont, Kit Carson, and their party, who first sighted the lake in 1844 from points southwest. When the Comstock silver lode was discovered near Virginia City in 1859, only a short distance east, the Bonanza Road became the first west-to-east road across the mountains, built to accommodate fortune hunters, who were trekking northerly Beckworth Pass and Donner Pass, and Carson Pass to the south, to cash in on the region's mineral wealth. To supply lumber for mines and settlements, a logging campaign sprang up, which stripped the Tahoe area of its rich conifer forests between 1860 and 1890. Dan De Quille, an editor at the *Virginia City Territorial Enterprise,* wrote, "The Comstock Lode may truthfully be said to be the tomb of the forests of the Sierras. Millions on millions of feet of lumber are annually buried in the mines, nevermore to be resurrected."

Mark Twain was not alone in his appreciation for the area's natural beauty. Other early visitors included George Wharton James, who wrote the rhapsodic *Lake Tahoe: Lake of the Sky* in 1915, and John Muir, whose trips to Yosemite and Lake Tahoe were among the inspirations that led him to found the Sierra Club in 1892 in San Francisco. As mining and logging depleted stores of natural wealth, a bonanza of leisure resorts took its place, catering to well-heeled San Franciscans looking for respite from the city. The Tallac House, Tahoe Tavern, and Glenbrook Inn provided lavish accommodation to visitors, who plied the lake by steamship, took in the area's bucolic vistas, and imbibed the rejuvenating effects of Tahoe's sanguine climate.

Lake Tahoe became one of the first areas to benefit from early efforts at environmental protection as local community leaders led efforts to replant forests and promote the natural beauty of the region as a national treasure. Efforts in 1912, 1913, and 1918 to designate the basin a national park, however, were unsuccessful. By automobile, Americans came in added numbers in the 1920s, which led to the building and paving of more roads, which led in turn to the building of more lodges and retreats. After the legalization of gambling in Nevada in 1931, casinos began springing up all over Tahoe's lakeside resort community on the Nevada side. Harvey's Wagon Wheel Saloon and Gambling Hall and the Cal-

Neva Resort on the North Shore—once owned by Frank Sinatra—were among the many popular venues.

Following World War II, Tahoe experienced a building boom and upsurge in population, and with the coming of the Squaw Valley Olympics in 1960, the region was placed squarely on the map. The number of permanent residents increased from 10,000 to 50,000, and summer residents from 10,000 to 90,000, over the next 20 years. From 1968 forward, as fear that the famous transparency of the lake's waters—with visibility to 75 feet in places—could be lost, concern for the protection of the Tahoe ecosystem began to dominate local policy. In the 1980s, development slowed after controls were placed on land use.

Today, the sparkling waters and treasured history of Lake Tahoe are a reminder of the broader narratives that have shaped and continue to shape the American West. The Tahoe area is host annually to millions of visitors, who come to ski and snow tube, hike the 165-mile Tahoe Rim Trail that circumnavigates the lake, relax at the lodges, try their luck at the casinos, or retreat to the serenity and repose afforded by the many area parks.

Checklist of Lake Tahoe Facts

- Tahoe is 22 miles long, 12 miles wide, has 72 miles of shoreline, and covers 191 square miles of surface area.
- Tallest area peaks are Freel Peak, at 10,881 feet; Monument Peak, at 10,067 feet; Pyramid Peak, at 9,983 feet; and Mount Tallac, at 9,735 feet—all composed of granite.
- Mount Pluto on the north is an extinct volcano that once created a natural dam for the lake.
- Tahoe is fed by 63 streams, but only the Lower Truckee River flows out, emptying into Pyramid Lake to the north.
- The Indian for Tahoe, "Da-ow-a-ga,"means "big water."
- Nestled at 6,229 feet above sea level between two peaks of the Sierra Nevada, Lake Tahoe has been measured at 1,645 feet at Crystal Bay, its deepest point.
- Average annual precipitation is 30 inches, including 216 inches of snow and 8.3 inches of rainfall.
- Lake volume is 39 trillion gallons and 700 years would be required for the lake to refill if it were drained.

- The lake never freezes because the waters are always in motion. At a depth of 600 feet, the waters are 39 degrees F year-round. At the surface, temperatures reach as high as 68 degrees F.
- The area is home to black bear, bald eagles, the yellow-headed blackbird, coyote, mule deer, Indian paintbrush, dwarf alpine aster, alder, aspen, and many other flora and fauna.
- Fannette Island is the lake's only island.
- The Ponderosa Ranch of TV's *Bonanza* is located on the Nevada side of the lake, as was the Corleone compound in *The Godfather: Part II*.
- The top 6 feet of the lake, used as a reservoir, are controlled by a dam on the Tahoe City end.
- Mark Twain accidentally started a forest fire here, according to chapter XXIII of his picaresque classic *Roughing It.*

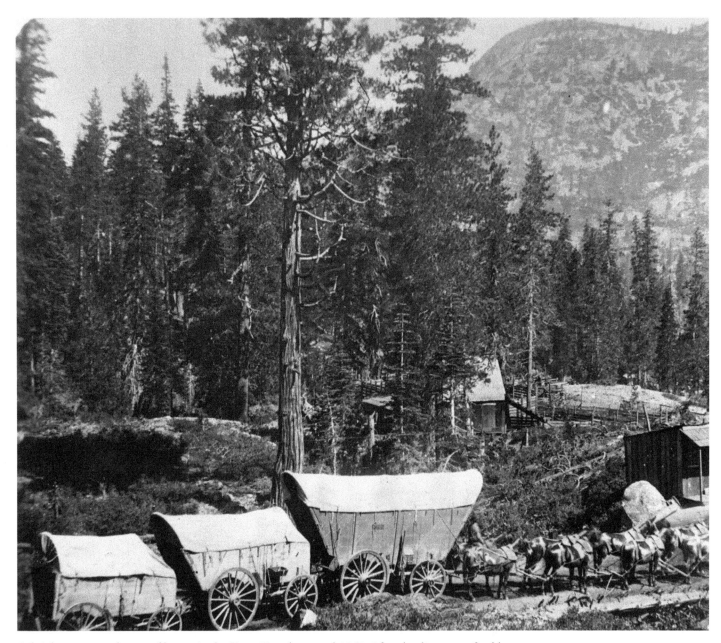

A freight wagon and team of horses in the Sierra Nevada around 1860. After the discovery of gold in California in 1849, trails across the Sierra Nevada became crowded with California-bound freight wagons and would-be miners who chose to brave the treacherous mountains rather than alternate routes around Cape Horn or across the Isthmus of Panama. Between twenty thousand and thirty thousand gold-seekers crossed the mountains north or south of Lake Tahoe.

EARLY DAYS AND PIONEER WAYS

(1860–1900)

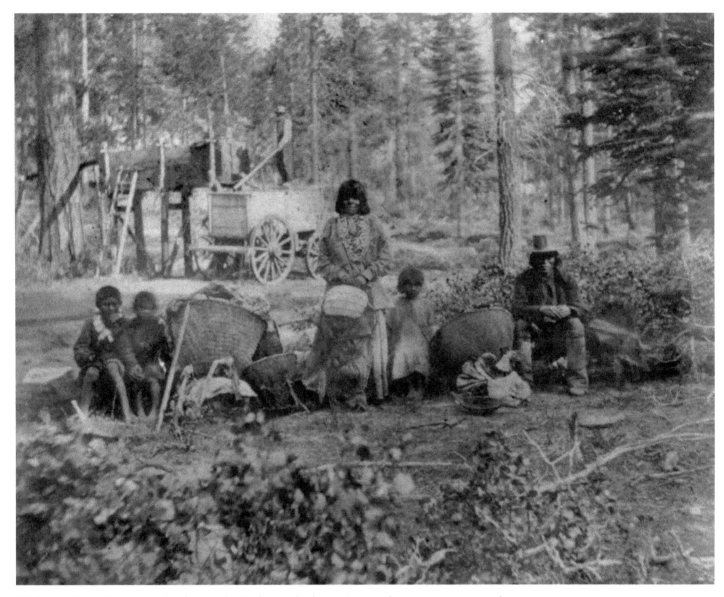

Washoe Indians. For thousands of years, the Washoe and other native peoples spent summers at the lake, establishing traditional campsites where they settled and held ceremonies during the warmer months of the year.

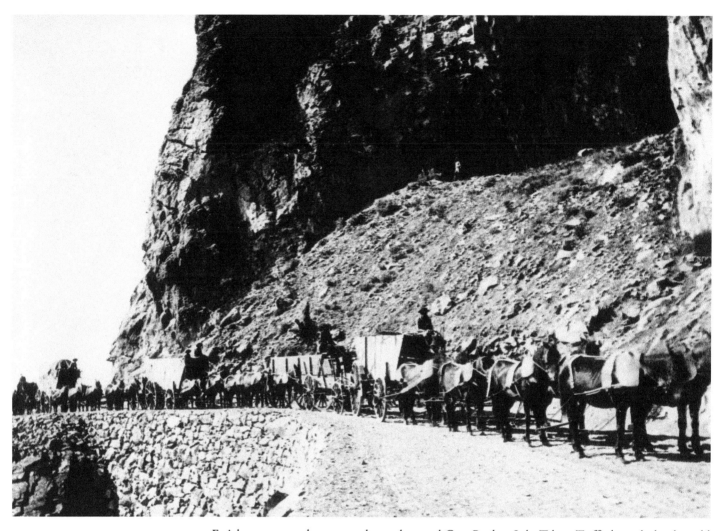

Freight wagons and teams on the road around Cave Rock at Lake Tahoe. Traffic brought by the gold rush led to the creation of new, well-maintained roads through the Sierra, often built privately and funded with tolls. The Johnson Cut-off, seen here, carried mail and supplies around the south end of the lake to what is now the Carson Valley.

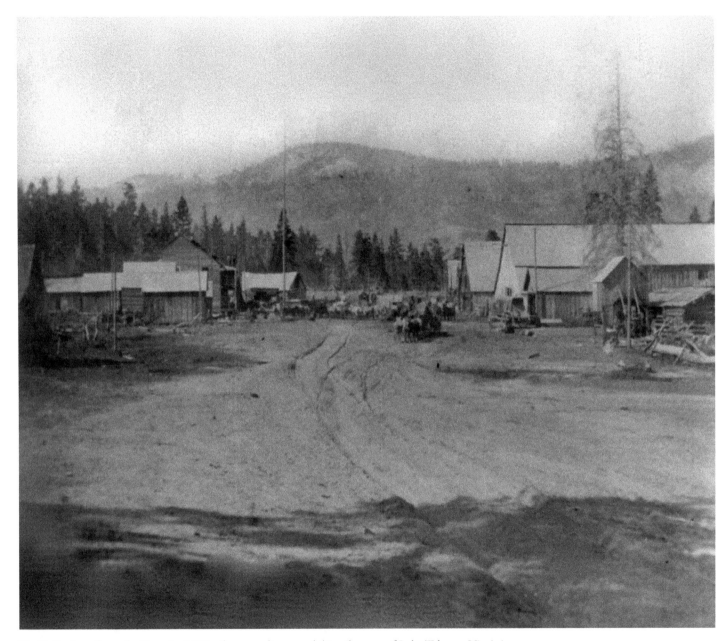

Yank's Station, from the East. In 1859, silver was discovered 40 miles east of Lake Tahoe—Virginia City's famous "Comstock Lode." The discovery brought a new rush of miners over the Sierra from California, and hotels, roadhouses, saloons, and trading posts sprang up to accommodate them. By 1865, the area around the lake boasted 10 to 15 hotels, public houses, and way stations; many offered beds, food, and gambling while nearby saloons provided liquor, women, and company.

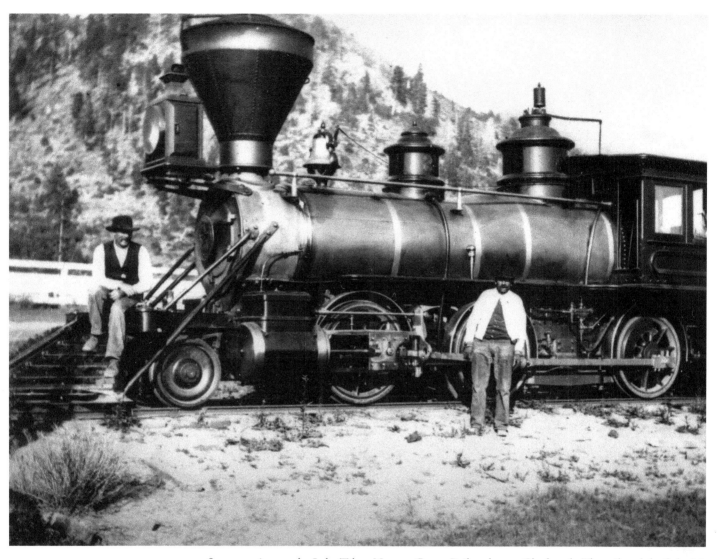

Steam engine on the Lake Tahoe Narrow Gauge Railroad, near Glenbrook. The railroad, built by H. M. Yerington and D. W. Bliss, carried timber from Lake Tahoe closer to Virginia City and its mines. The track was eight-and-three-quarters miles long, running from Glenbrook on the Nevada side of the lake to the eastern summit of the Sierra Nevada.

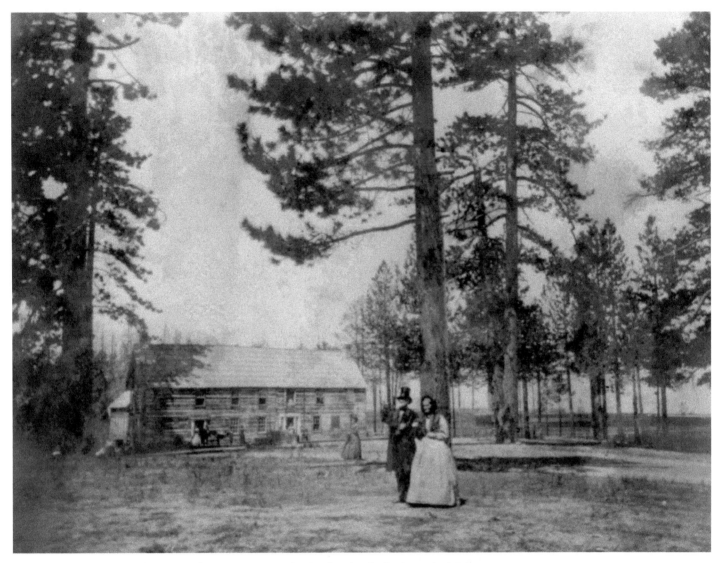

The Lake House, erected from hewn logs in 1860, was the first hotel to be built on the lake's shore. It was located on a less-traveled route along the lake's south shore, and though rumors of a transcontinental railroad that was to be built through Lake Valley never came to fruition, the hotel enjoyed great success before it burned to the ground in 1866.

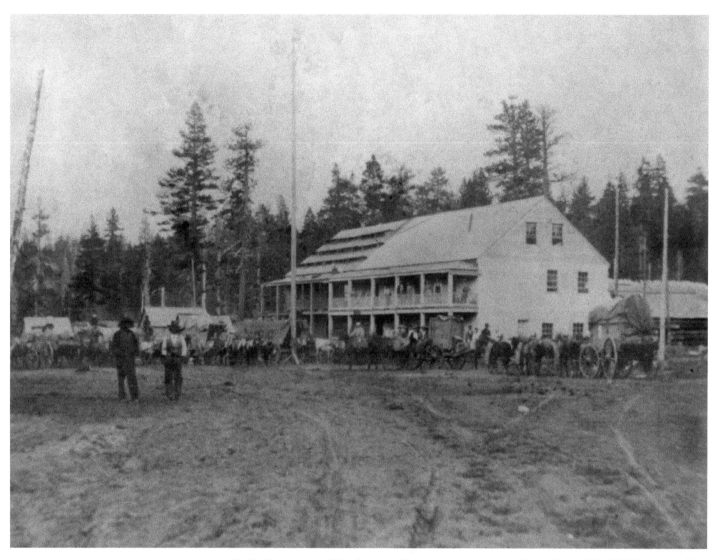

Yank's Station, established as a trading post, was purchased by Ephraim "Yank" Clement and his wife, Lydia, in 1859. They turned the stage stop into a 3-story, 14-room hotel with a large barn and corrals. A town sprang up around the popular way station, including several saloons, a farmer's co-op, a blacksmith shop, a general store, and a meat processing plant.

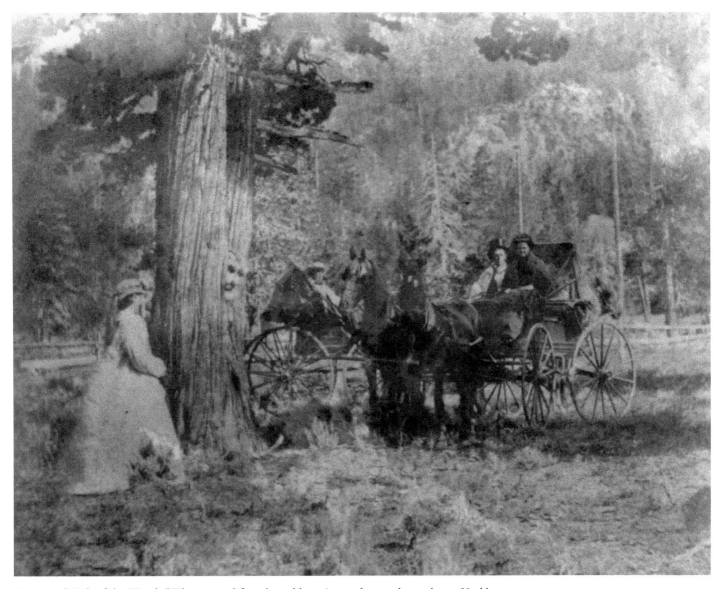

A visit to "Nick of the Woods." The unusual face-shaped knot in a cedar tree located near Yank's Station was a popular attraction for passing travelers.

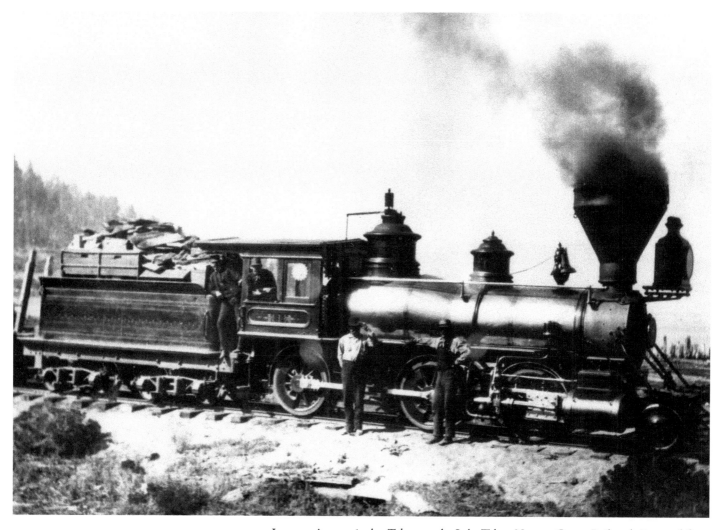

Locomotive no. 1, the *Tahoe,* on the Lake Tahoe Narrow Gauge Railroad. Demand for a transcontinental railroad connecting California with the rest of the nation was finally met in 1869 with the completion of the Central Pacific Railroad, which passed through Truckee, California. Around the same time, local entrepreneurs looking to expedite delivery of lumber to Virginia City began building narrow-gauge railroads throughout the Tahoe basin.

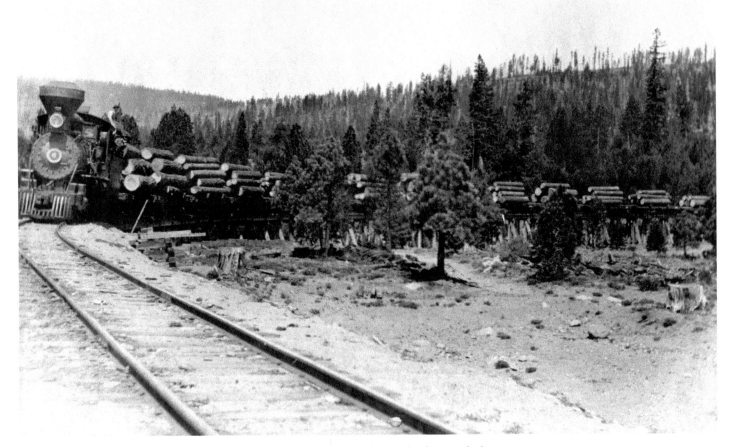

A train loaded with logs crosses a trestle in the forest. The Comstock silver rush, along with the construction of the Central Pacific Railroad, created a demand on Lake Tahoe's forests that removed nearly all the virgin timber from the basin.

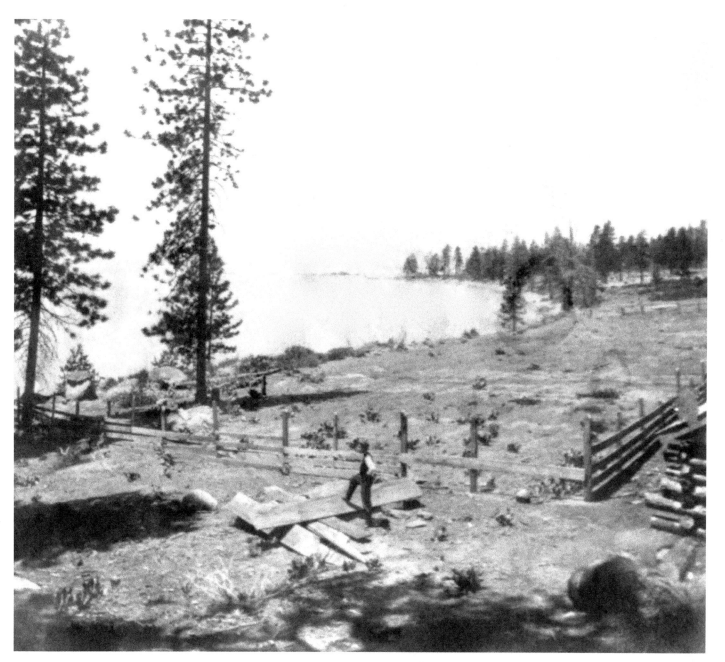

View from the Logan House, on the eastern shore, facing north.

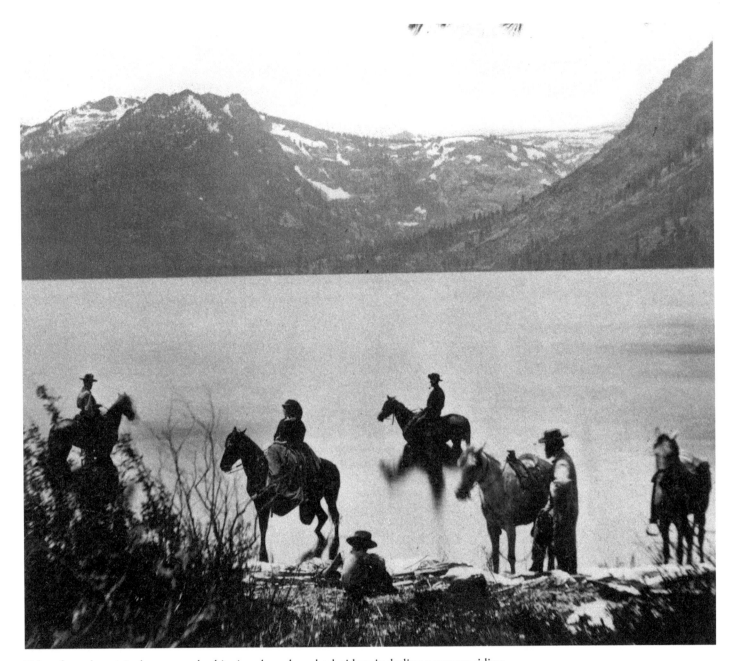

Taken from the original stereograph, this view shows horseback riders, including a woman riding sidesaddle, near the shore of Fallen Leaf Lake, a three-mile-long lake discovered by J. C. Johnson in 1853. Water from nearby springs was bottled and sold to health-conscious customers in San Francisco and Reno and became very popular during the 1880s.

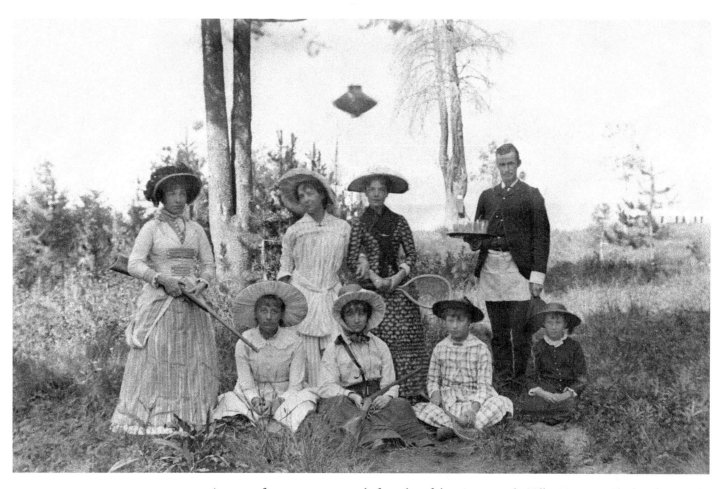

A group of young women, ready for a day of shooting, near the Tallac House in Glenbrook, Nevada. Known as the most elegant hotel in the area, Lucky Baldwin's Tallac House boasted archery fields, a telegraph office, lawns for croquet, and formal-dress dining rooms. The fellow at right holds a tray of refreshments.

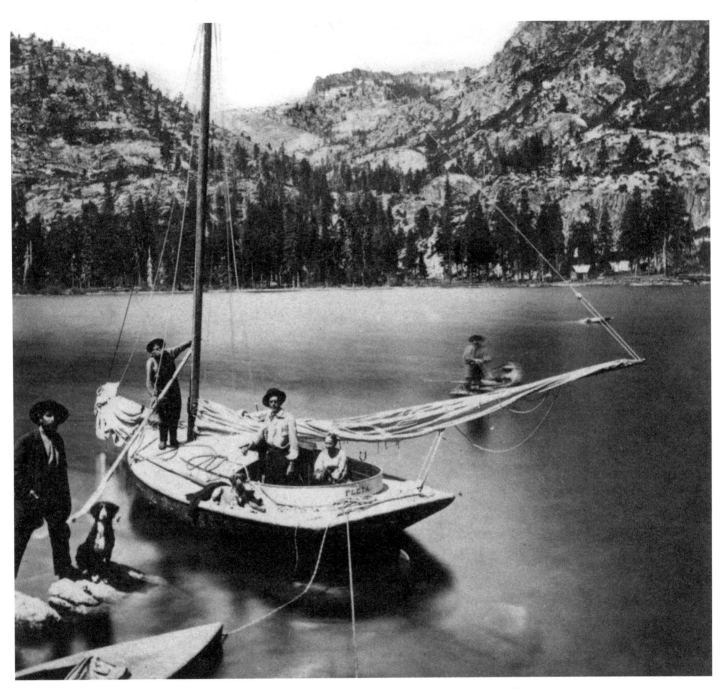

A view of boats on the western shore of Lake Tahoe near Eagle Canyon, from Eckley's Island, Emerald Bay. After 1850, sailboats began to be brought to the lake or built on-site for recreational use.

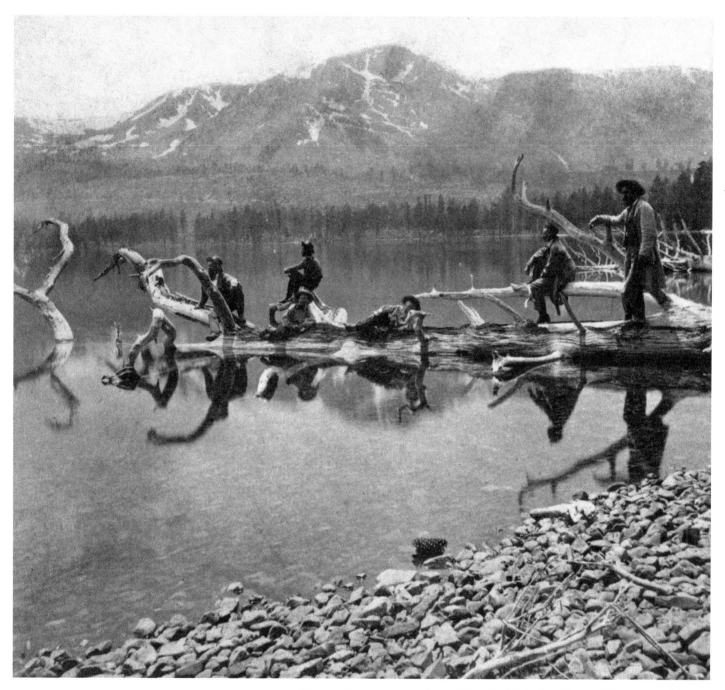

Men and boys pose on a log at Fallen Leaf Lake for this carefully composed image.

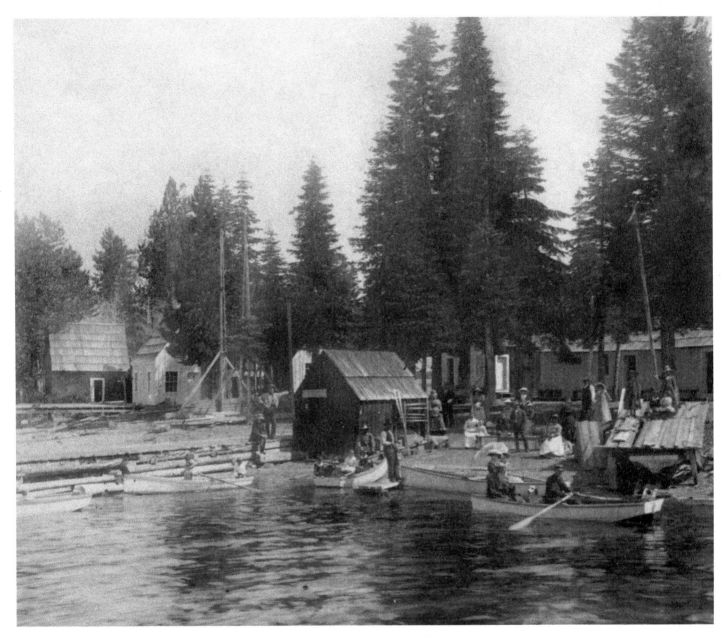

McKinney's Landing, located on the west shore north of Sugar Pine Point, was built in 1863 to cater to outdoorsmen wanting to hunt, camp, and fish in the wilderness and experience the rugged "mountain man" life-style. By 1875, the rustic hunting lodge had expanded to include a clubhouse, bar, boat house, and pier to accommodate steamers.

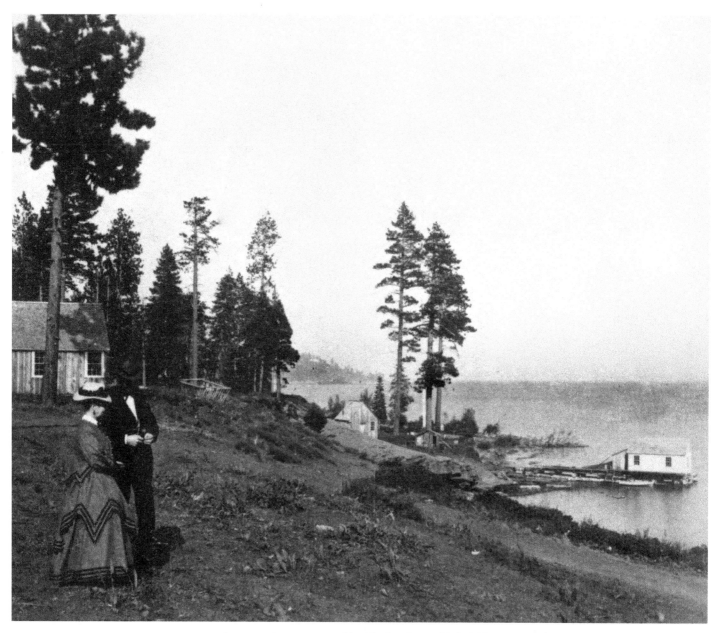

A man and woman stand beside the shore of Lake Tahoe, near Tahoe City on the northwest shore. Tahoe City grew up around the Tahoe City Hotel during the 1860s and was dependent in its early days on water transportation and one rough trail through a canyon to Truckee, 50 miles away. The grand opening of the remodeled hotel was celebrated with a cruise around the lake on the new steamer *Governor Blasdel.*

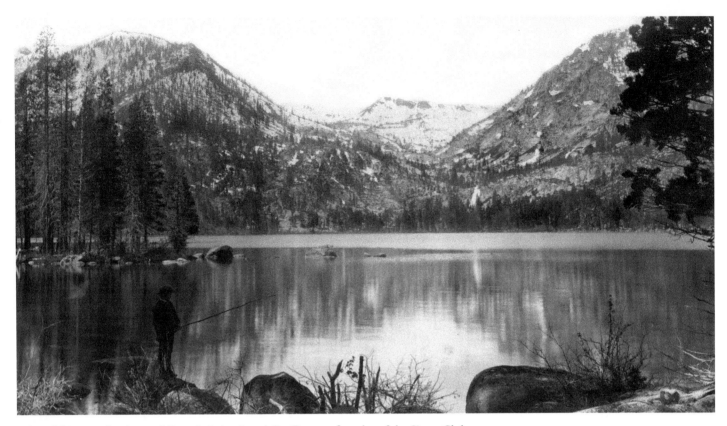

A boy fishing on the shore of Cascade Lake. Joseph Le Conte, a founder of the Sierra Club, wrote in 1870 while camped at South Shore, "Of all the places I have yet seen, this one I could enjoy the longest and love the most."

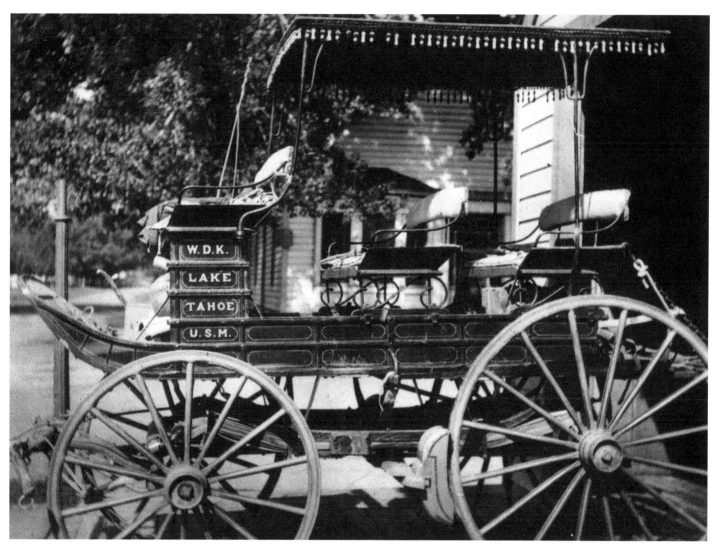

An eight-passenger station wagon. The initials W. D. K. stood for William D. Keyser.

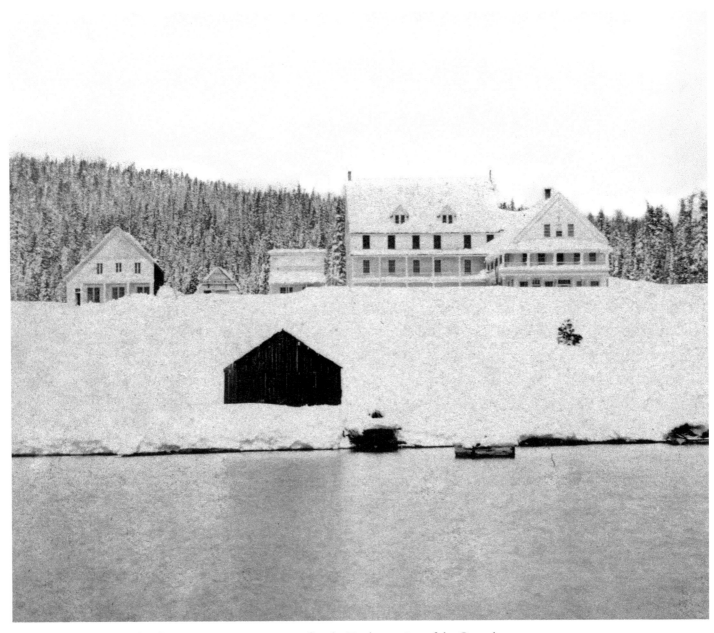

The Grand Central Hotel, Tahoe City. In 1870, two years after the Truckee station of the Central Pacific Railroad opened, the Tahoe City Hotel was remodeled and named the Grand Central. The hotel's posh dining room could accommodate up to 150 visitors and soon was regularly filled to capacity.

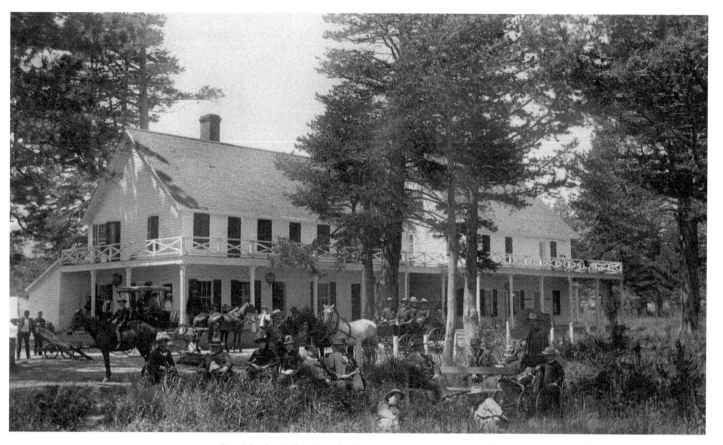

Outside the Tallac Hotel, where hotel guests and possibly hotel staff pose for a group portrait. The popular, expensive hotel offered amenities such as velvet drapes, and entertained guests with hikes in the surrounding wilderness, picnics, horseback rides, and fishing trips, among other activities.

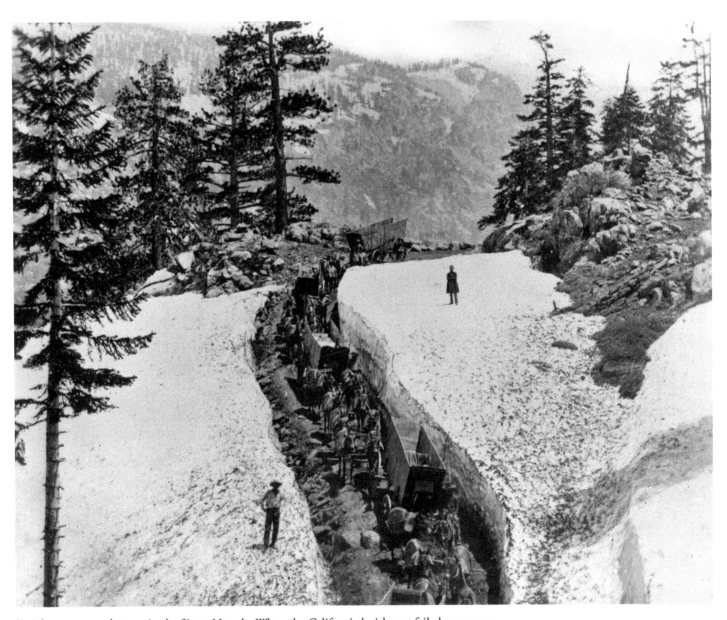

Freight wagons and teams in the Sierra Nevada. When the California legislature failed to approve funding for a road across the mountains that would connect California with the east, local investors quickly constructed a series of toll roads through the lake valley to accommodate those heading to the mines. Travelers passing through the valley might have to pay up to 10 different tolls in order to complete their journey. Toll roads were a far cry from the treacherous route that doomed the Donner Party, but the passage was still hazardous.

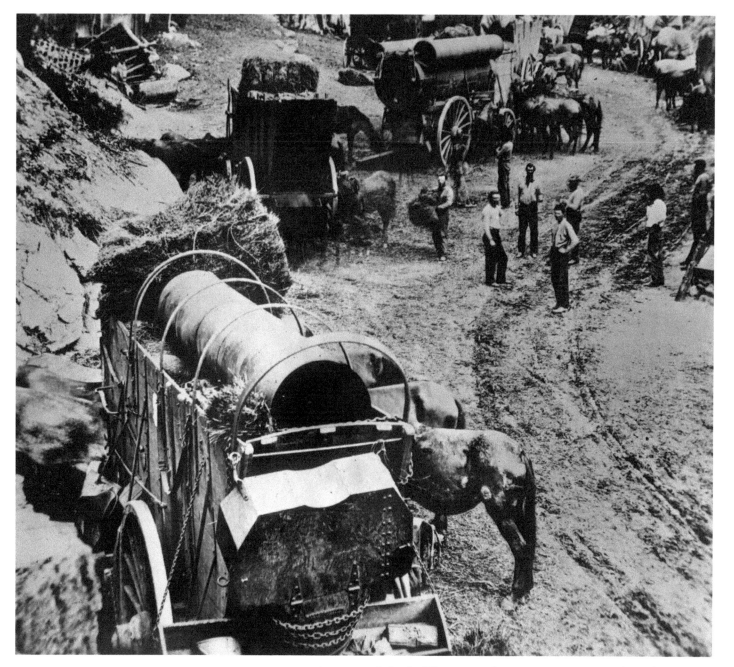

A wagon train in the Tahoe area makes a rest stop on its way through the Sierra.

Freight wagons and teams at a way station near Glenbrook, Nevada. Glenbrook, on the eastern shore of the lake, became a center of operations for the region's booming lumber trade.

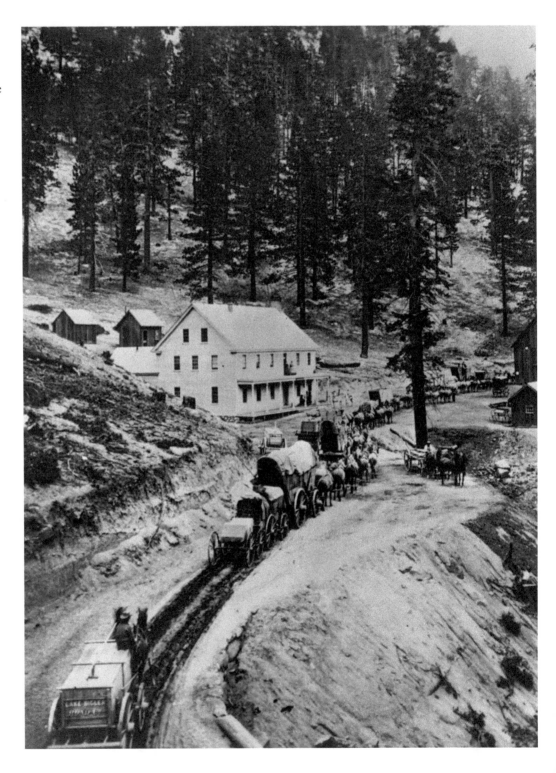

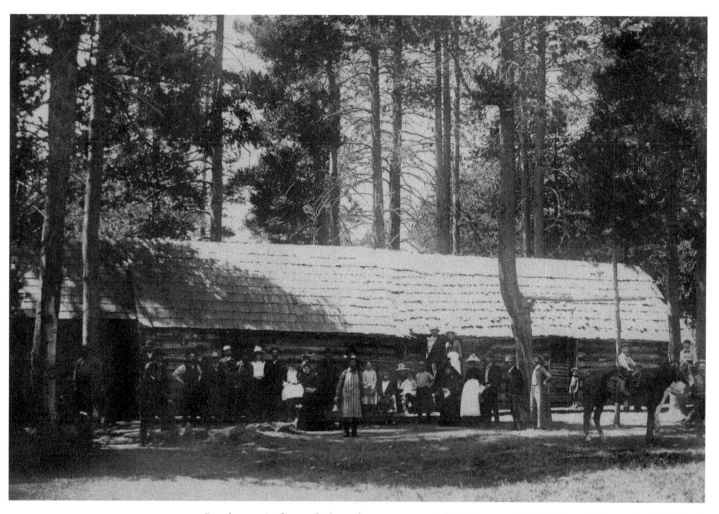

People pose in front of a log cabin resort near Lake Tahoe, probably Rubicon Springs. Locals claimed that carbonated water taken from the springs was "better than whiskey," but there was no way other than mule train to transport it down the mountain until 1886, when Mrs. Phillips Clark bought the land, opened a 16-room hotel and health spa, and persuaded the county to build the Rubicon Road. The hotel was popular, owing in part to Mrs. Clark's reputation as "best cook in the Sierra."

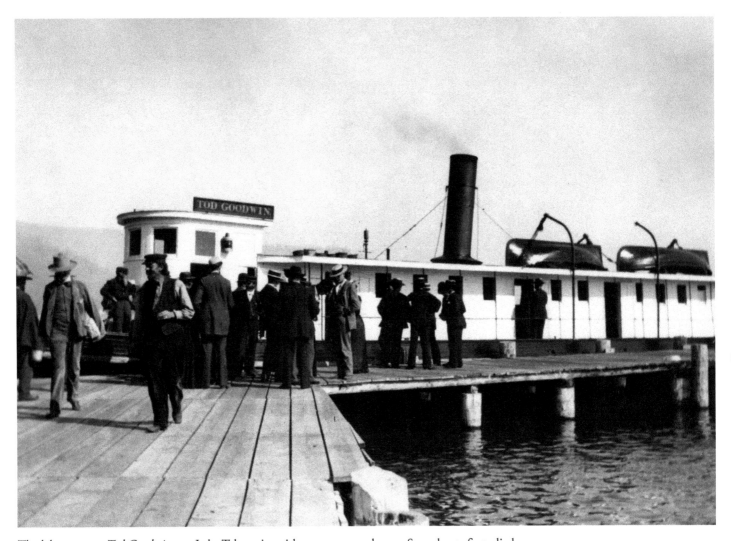

The lake steamer *Tod Goodwin* at a Lake Tahoe pier with passengers and crew. Steamboats first plied the lake for use in logging operations and freight delivery. As the Comstock played out and the lake became more of a tourist destination, they gained increasing popularity as a means of transportation for visitors to resorts around the lake.

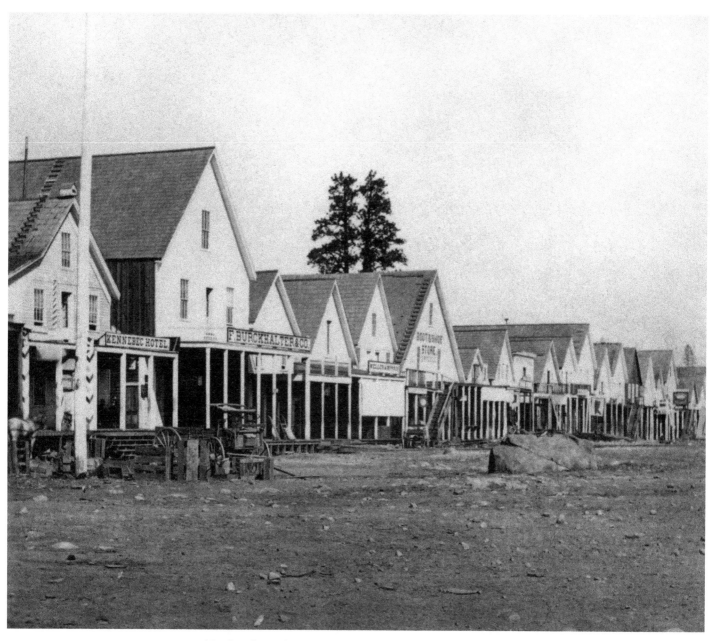

Truckee, located 12 miles northwest of the lake's northern shore, was the nearest stop on the Central Pacific Railroad. Though it bypassed the Tahoe basin, the coming of the transcontinental railroad in 1869 provided easy access to the lake and forever established tourism as an industry there.

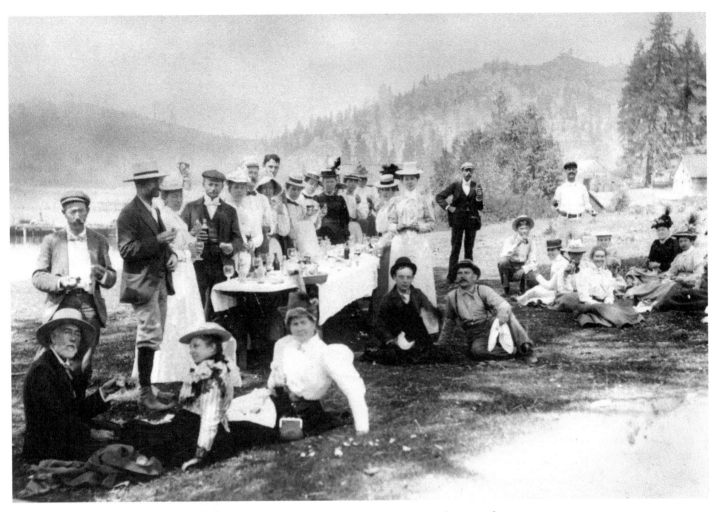

A group of picnickers on the beach at Lake Tahoe. As the nineteenth century progressed, more of the lake's visitors came seeking pleasure rather than riches. Wealthy mine tycoons from Virginia City, escaping the heat and noise of the mining boomtown, flooded elegant hotels along the lake's shores during the summer. Posh resorts and the new railroad would later attract more visitors from San Francisco and farther away.

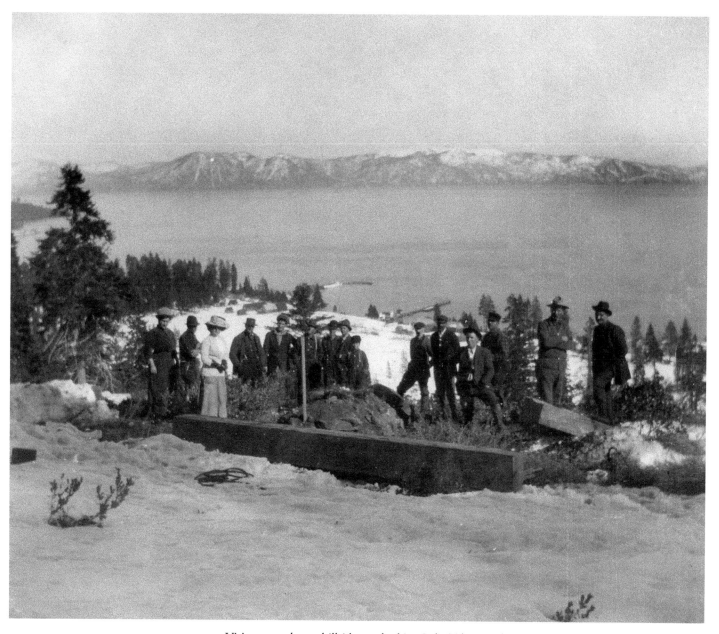

Visitors stand on a hillside overlooking Lake Tahoe, with piers on the lake visible in the distance. Hiking and skiing in the mountains were popular activities. To help people explore, enjoy, and protect the Sierra Nevada wilderness, naturalist John Muir founded the Sierra Club in 1892.

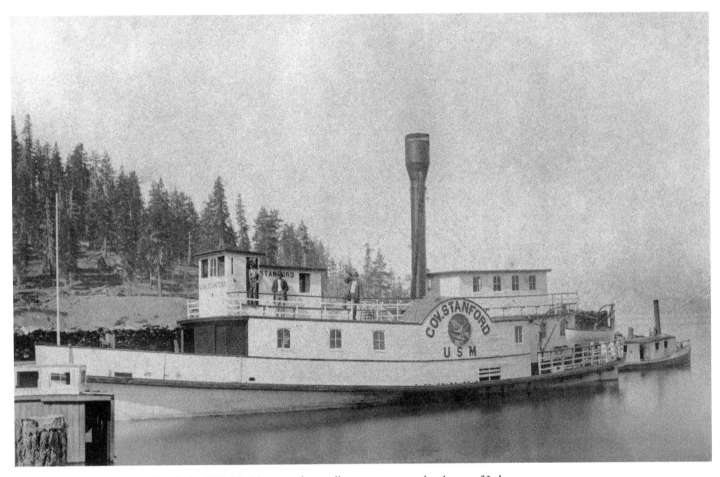

The lake steamer *Governor Stanford,* a U.S. Mail boat, and a smaller steamer near the shores of Lake Tahoe. The *Governor Stanford* was built as the silver rush wound down and sailed the lake for only 10 years.

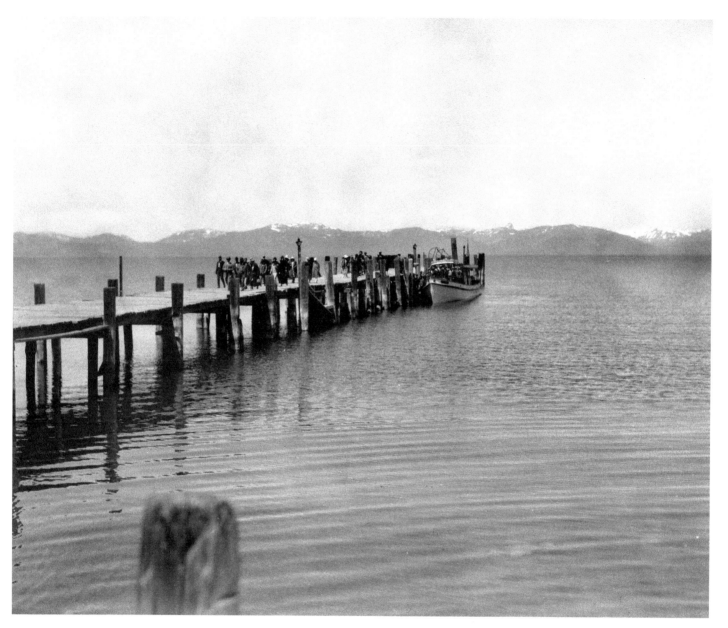

A steamer unloads passengers at a pier.

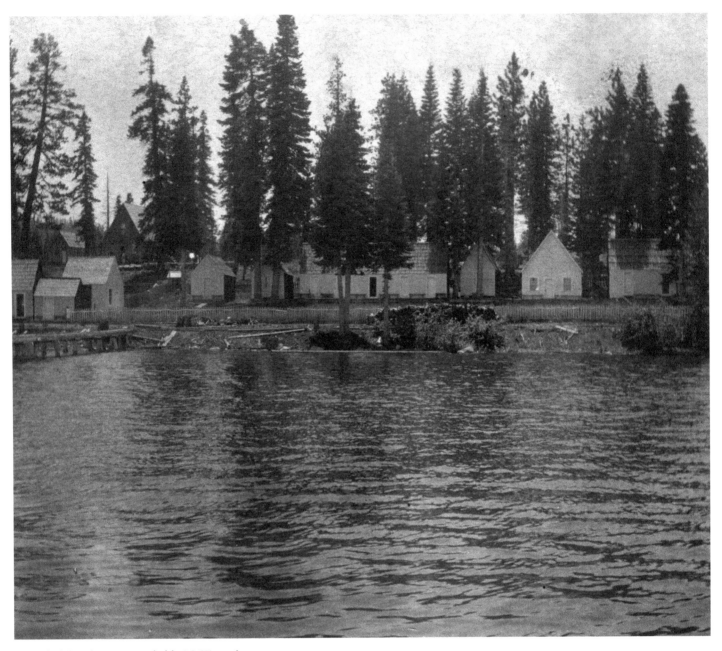

An early lakeside resort, probably McKinney's.

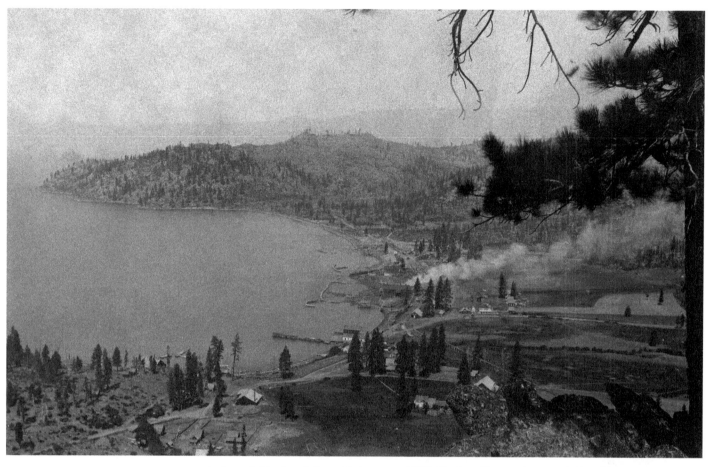

A view of Glenbrook from Shakespeare Cliff. Glenbrook's growth coincided with that of the logging industry, and during its height four sawmills were in constant operation around the settlement. In this view, hills that were once thickly forested show a sparse supply of trees.

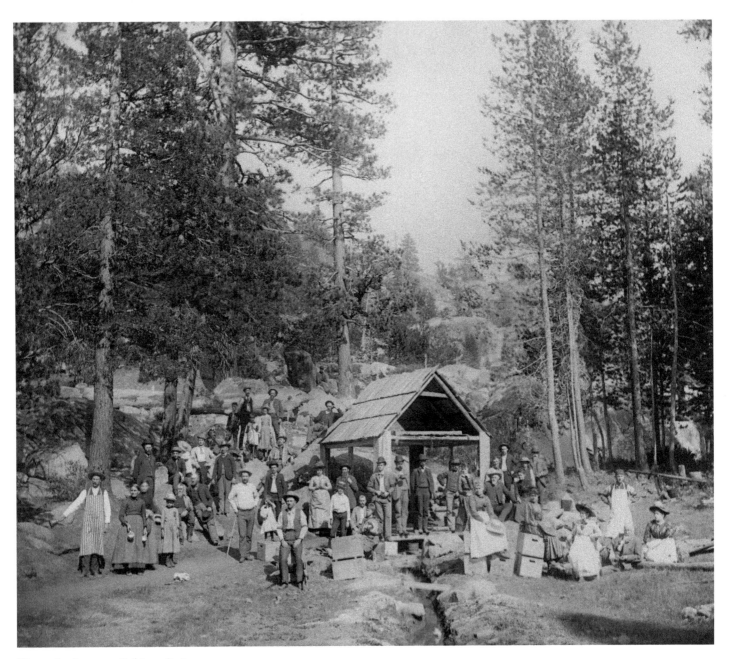

The spring house at Rubicon Springs.

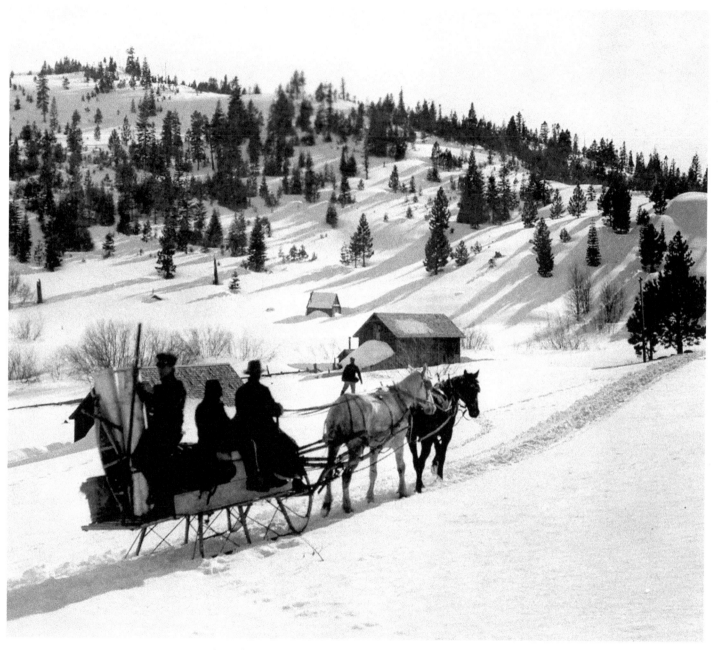

Travelers in a wide-runner sleigh climb from Carson City, Nevada, to Lake Tahoe. The horses were harnessed tandem and, after 1910, sometimes in snowshoes.

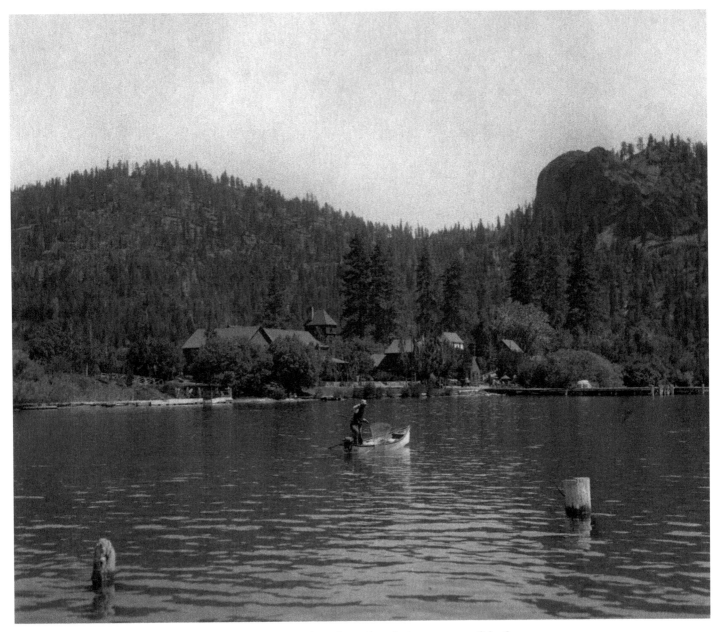

A fisherman gets a strike in front of the Glenbrook Inn. Built in the 1860s, the inn was one of the first luxury hotels on the shores of the lake.

FROM SILVER LODES TO GOLDEN LODGES

(1901–1920)

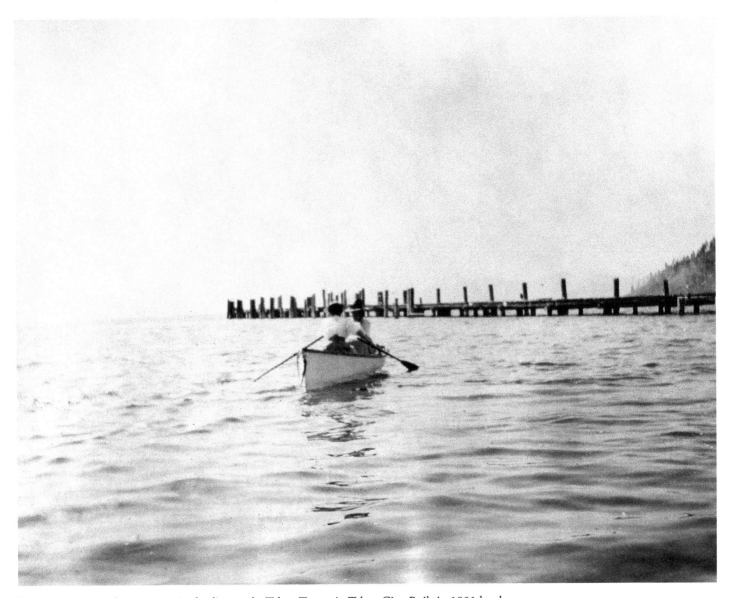

Two women row a boat near a pier leading to the Tahoe Tavern in Tahoe City. Built in 1901 by the Bliss family, the Tahoe Tavern was a first-class metropolitan hotel touted as one of the region's most prestigious watering holes.

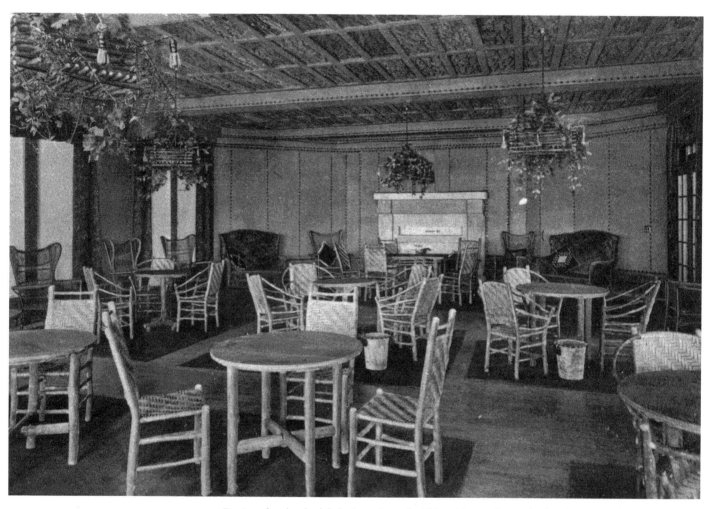

Designed to be the lake's showplace, the Tahoe Tavern featured a bowling alley, casino, ballroom, shuffleboard court, and barber shop. Shown here is a part of the casino.

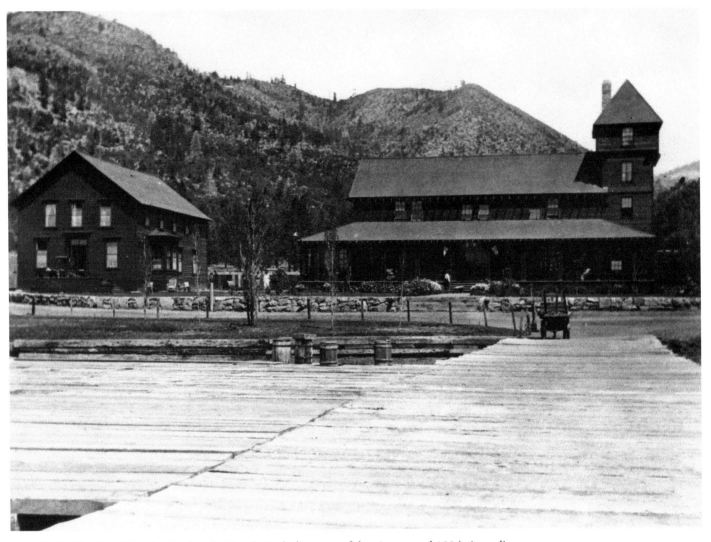

Outside the Glenbrook Inn in Glenbrook, Nevada, including part of the pier, around 1904. According to hotel owners, guests of the Glenbrook included General William T. Sherman and presidents Ulysses S. Grant and Rutherford B. Hayes.

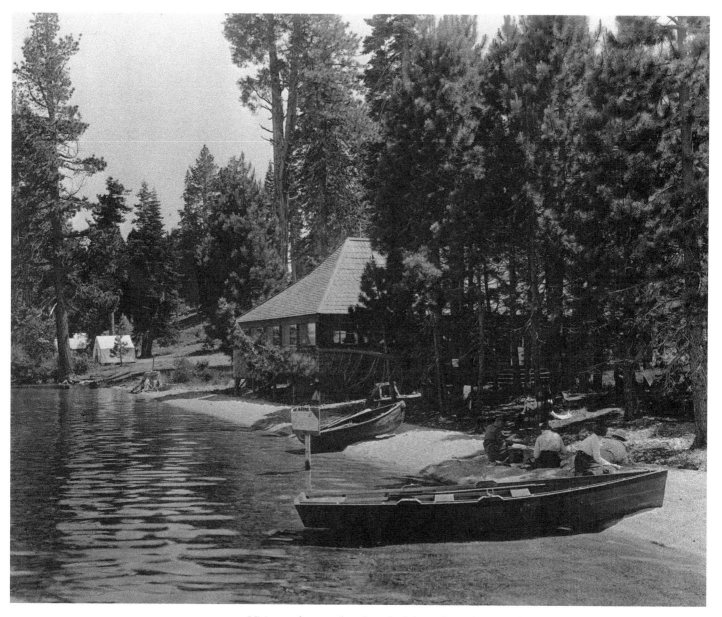

Visitors relax on a beach at the lake with rowboats in the foreground, tents and cabins in the background.

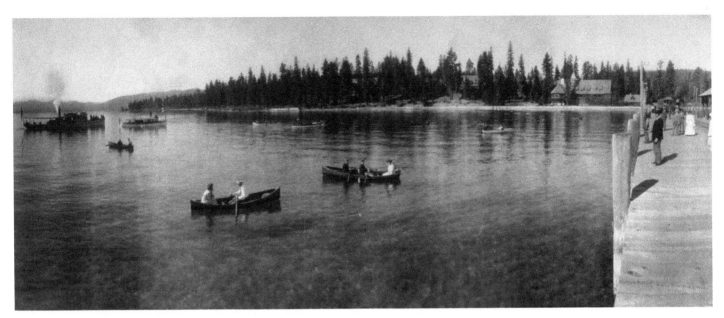

A boardwalk in front of the Tahoe Tavern, where a train approaches in the background and the *Tahoe* plies the waters at left. Duane L. Bliss, the builder of the hotel, built a narrow-gauge railroad between Truckee and Tahoe City to meet Southern Pacific trains and bring travelers back to the lake. Luminaries such as Henry Ford and Thomas Edison were among the visitors. He also built the passenger steamer *Tahoe,* providing what was at the time the most comfortable and reliable way to travel around the lake and ensuring a steady stream of visitors to the Tahoe Tavern.

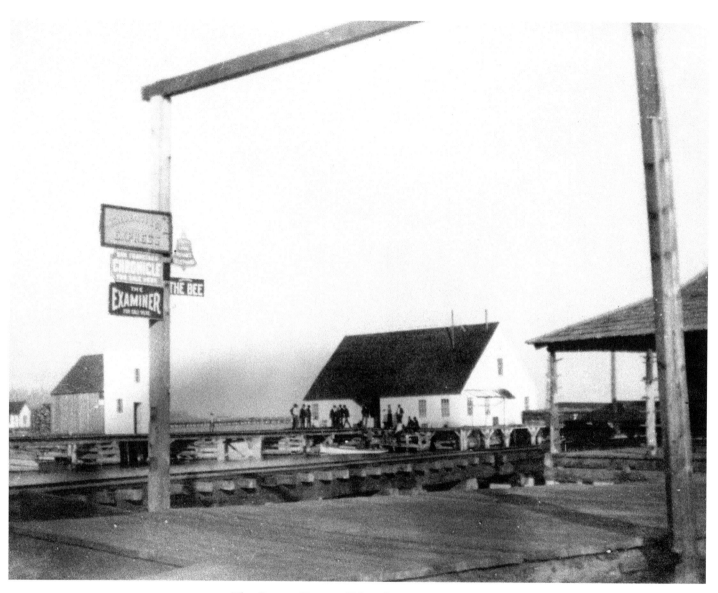

The Custom House at Tahoe City was a post office and 24-hour waterfront saloon offering two billiards parlors, one reserved for ladies.

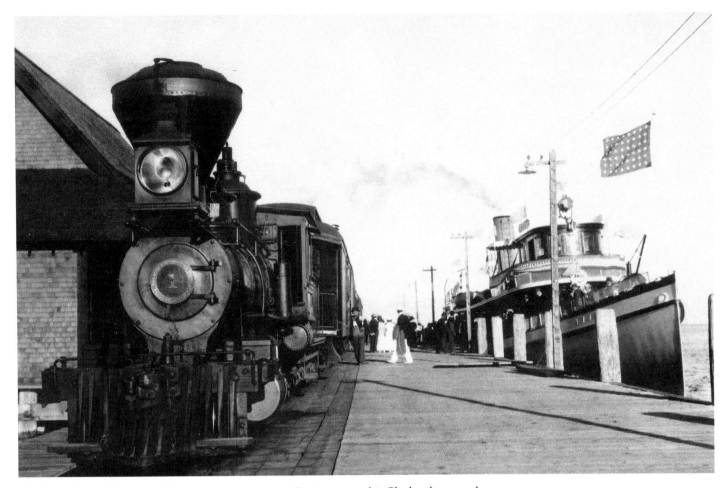

The Lake Tahoe Railway and Transportation Company Engine no. 1, the *Glenbrook,* meets the steamer *Tahoe* at the pier in Tahoe City. The *Tahoe* was the grandest ship on the lake, sporting polished brass fittings, a teak and mahogany deckhouse, leather upholstery, a dining hall, a smoking lounge, and marble lavatory fixtures with hot and cold running water. It was designed to accommodate 200 passengers, along with baggage and freight, in luxurious comfort.

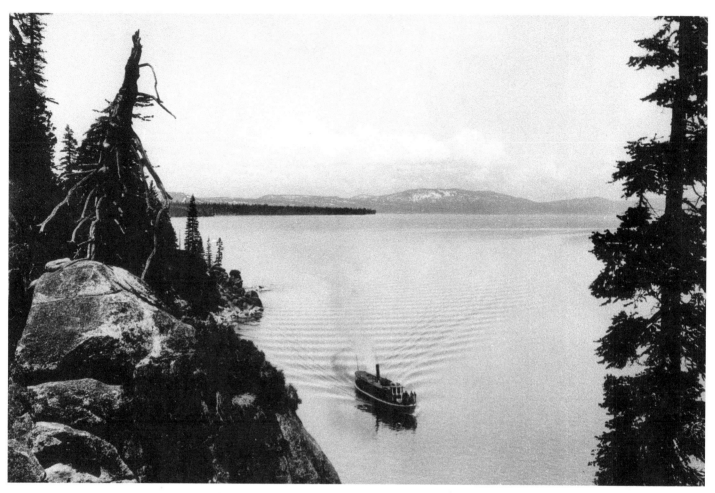

The steamer *Nevada* passes Rubicon Point. Owned by Tallac House owner Lucky Baldwin, the *Nevada* could accommodate up to 40 passengers in style and comfort.

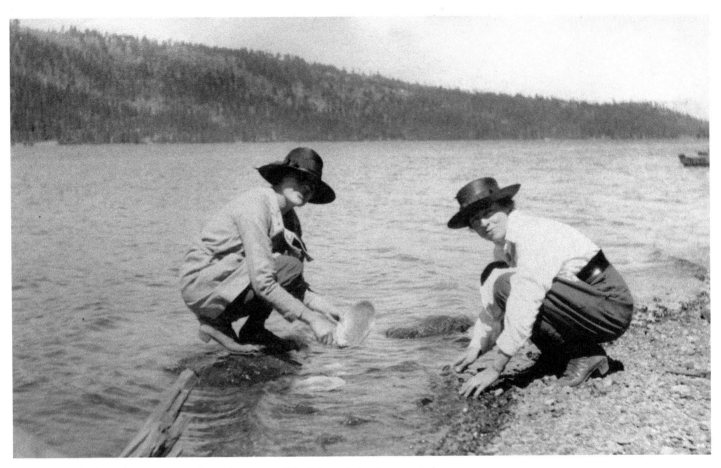

Campers scrub their plates and utensils in the waters of the lake early in the twentieth century.

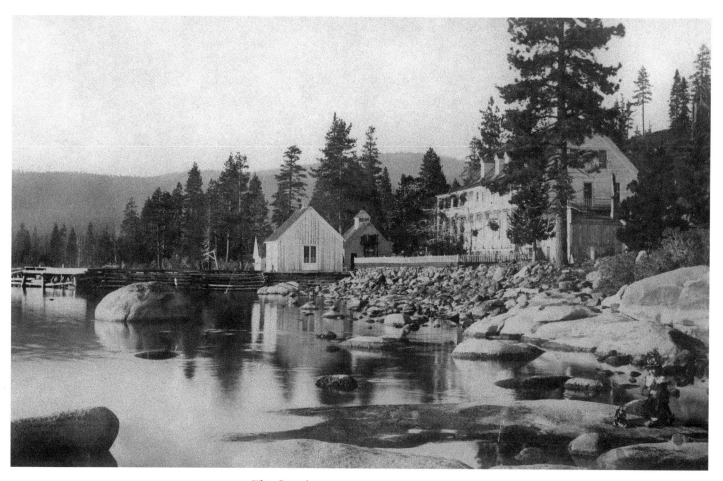

The Carnelian Hot Springs Hotel. Health spas and mineral springs were popular during the nineteenth century, and the Tahoe area provided many natural hot mineral springs. Dr. Bourne's Hygienic Establishment was built at Carnelian Bay in 1871, north of Tahoe City, and later renamed Carnelian Springs Sanatoria, for the semi-precious stones found there. It advertised fresh air, a restful environment, and the healing properties of the mineral springs.

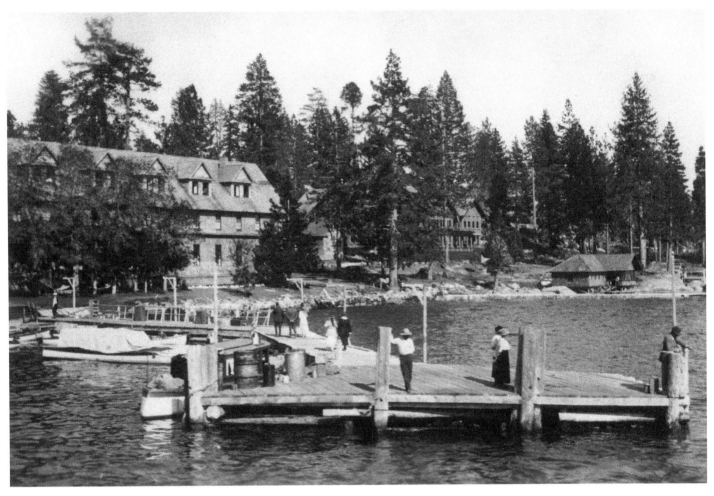

Tahoe Tavern, to the left, beside Pleasure Wharf. Tahoe Tavern became one of the luxury resorts at the lake notorious for operating illegal casino games.

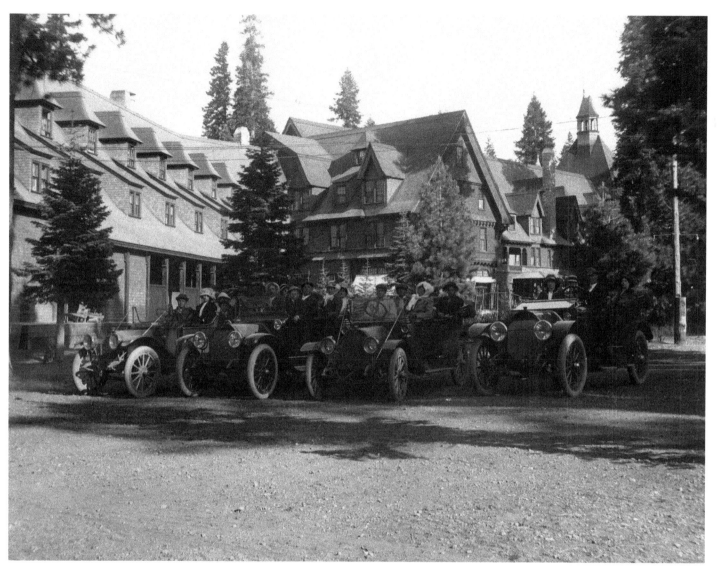

Automobiles line up in front of the Tahoe Tavern. The hotel promoted motor excursions to the lake and awarded a trophy to the first car of the season to drive over the new, yet still rugged, state highway 40 north of the lake.

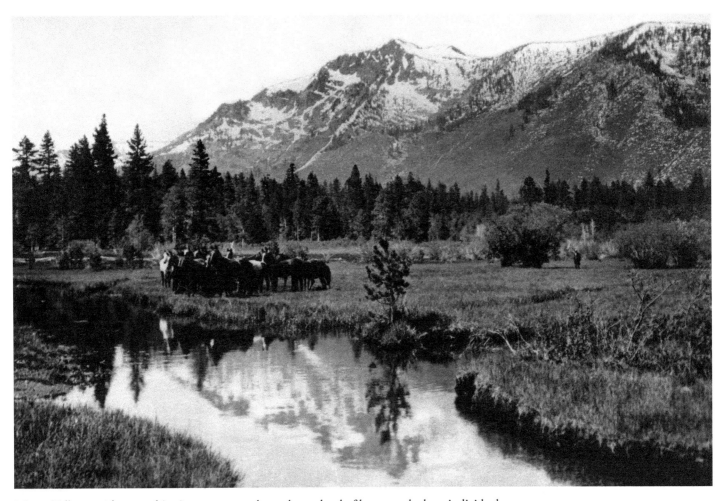

Mount Tallac presides over this picturesque meadow, where a herd of horses and a lone individual stand for their photograph.

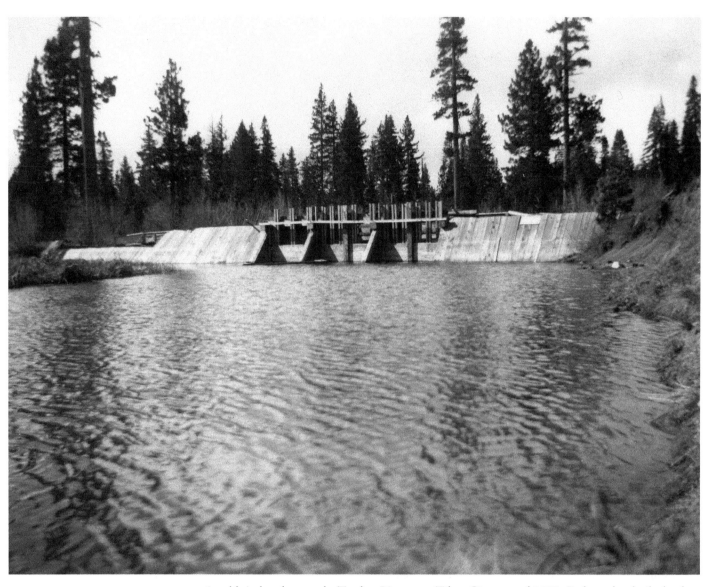

An old timber dam on the Truckee River, near Tahoe City, around 1902. Early settlers built the dam and bridge across the outlet to control the level of the lake.

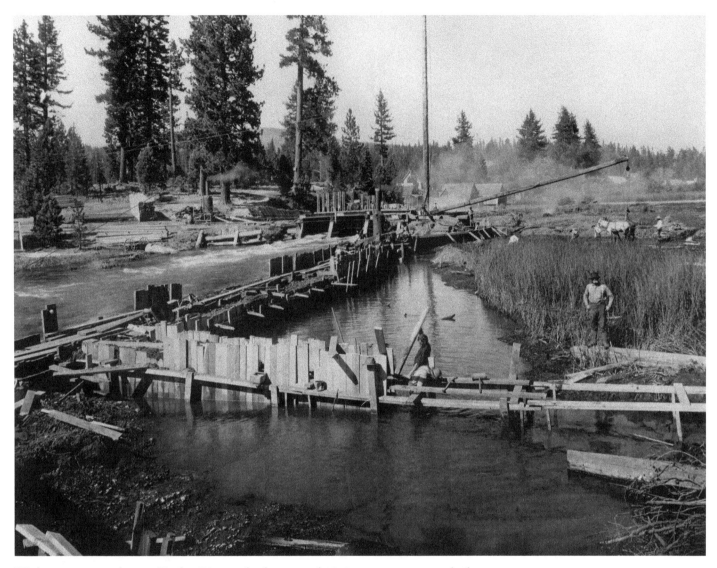

Work progresses on the new Truckee River outlet dam around 1912, a cement structure built to replace the older log and dirt dam. Owing to contractual complications, it remained unfinished until the fall of 1913. Today, this dam controls the level of the top six feet of the lake.

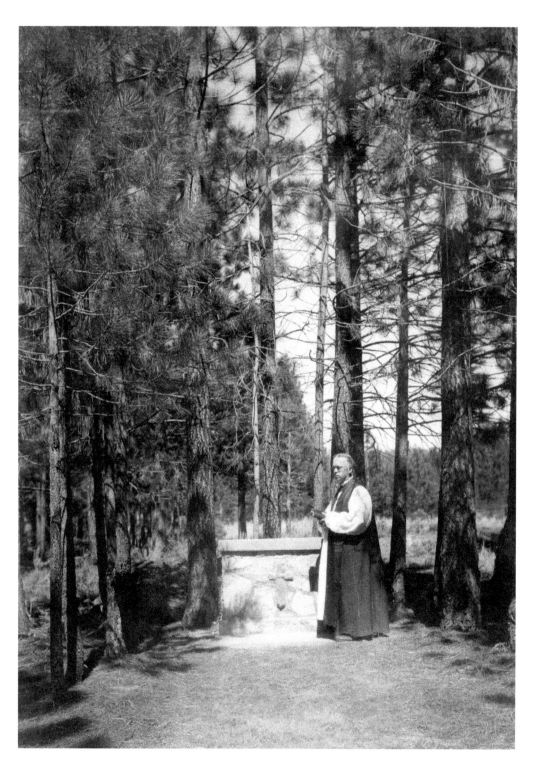

Episcopalian bishop George Coolidge Hunting, the third Bishop of Nevada, from 1914 to 1924, stands at an altar in the forest at the Episcopal Camp Galilee.

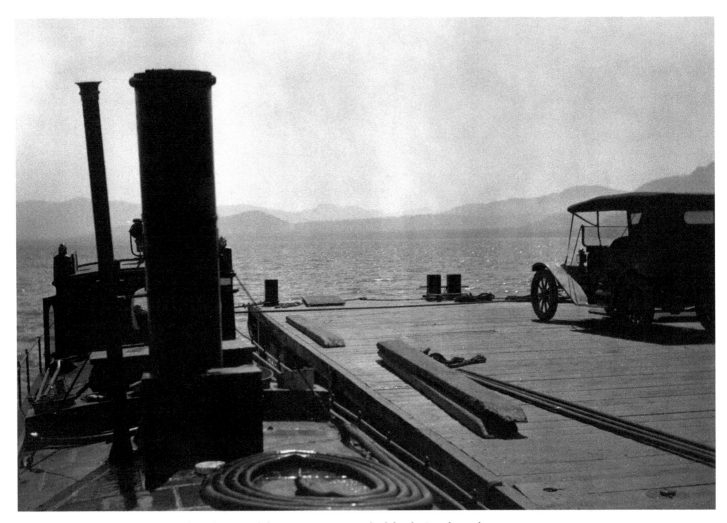

The convergence of steamship, rail, and automobile transportation to the lake during the early twentieth century helped drive the increase of tourism to the region.

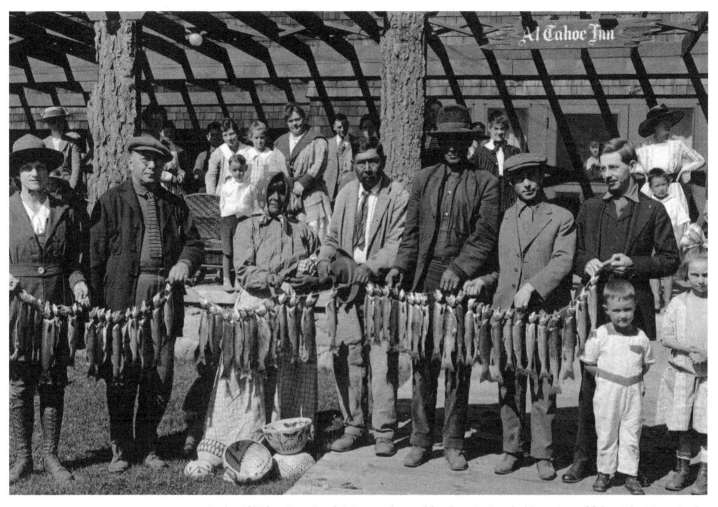

At the Al Tahoe Inn, Sarah Mayo and, possibly, Captain Pete hold a string of fish, with visitors in the background. Washoe baskets, visible in the foreground, are also on display.

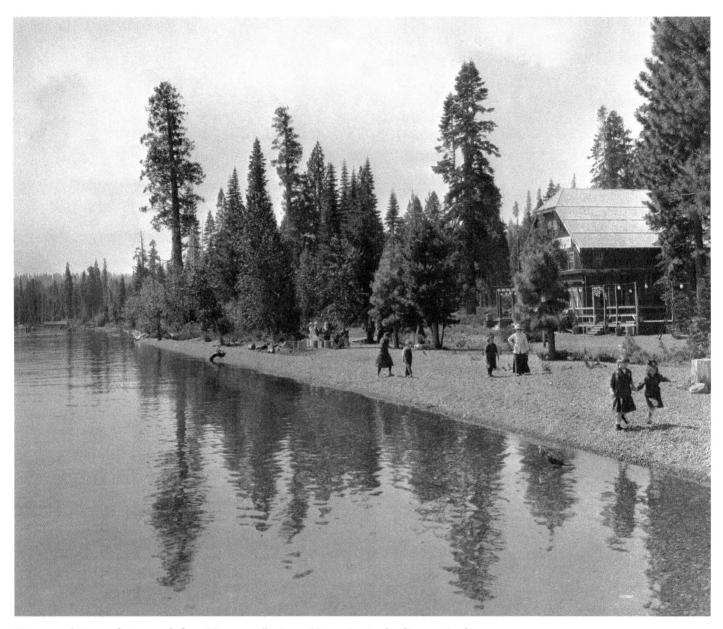

Homewood Resort, facing south from Homewood's pier to Upson Bay in the distance, in the summer of 1916. Women and children stroll along the beach. Homewood, like many settlements along the shores of the lake, thrived as a summer resort.

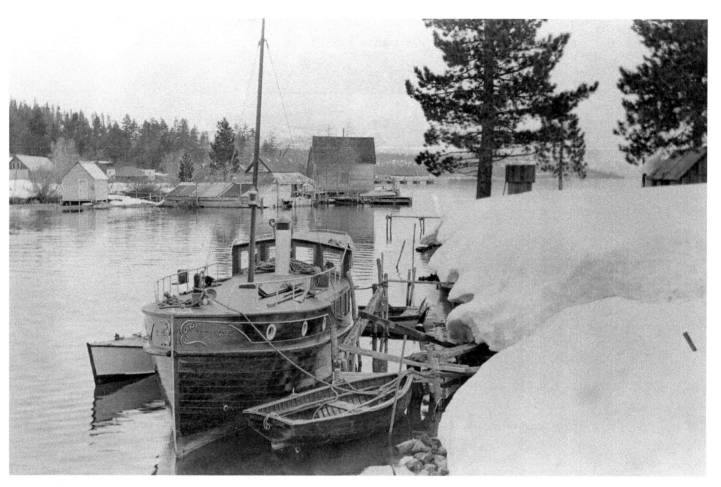

The three vessels of the Mount Rose snow survey, including the cabin cruiser *Mount Rose,* in a winter harbor at Lake Tahoe. University of Nevada, Reno, Professor James Edward Church devised a system for predicting seasonal water flow from precipitation stored as snow pack and established the nation's first high-altitude meteorological observatory on Mount Rose in 1905. His system is still used throughout the world today.

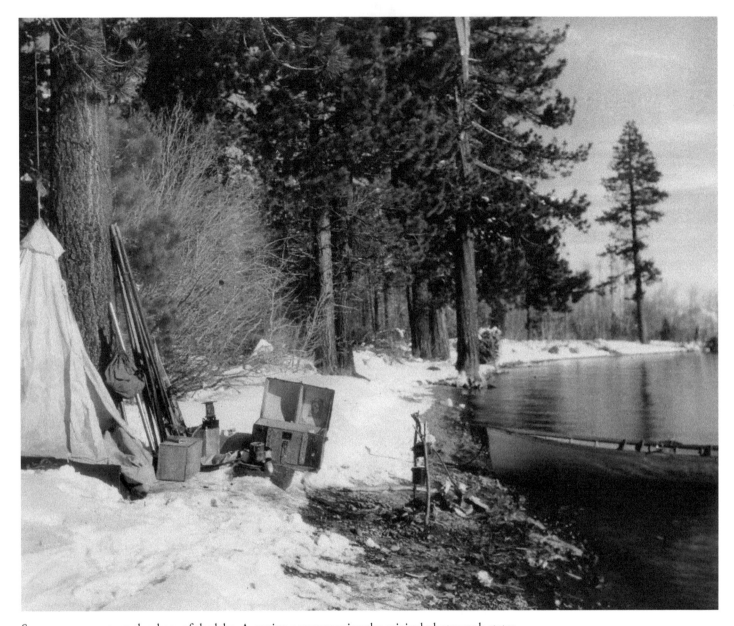

Snow survey camp on the shore of the lake. A caption accompanying the original photograph states that "the lake never freezes and, therefore, affords ready transportation by boat to all points on its shore line of 72 miles."

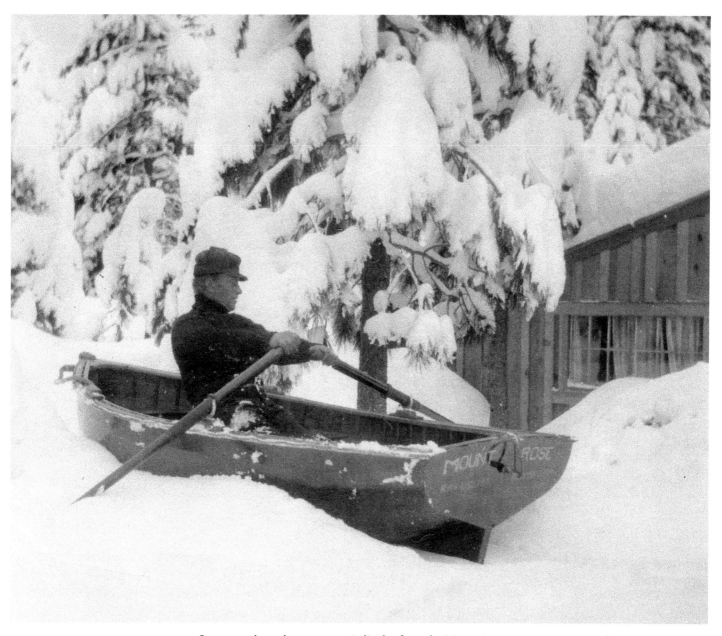

Some people are born to row. A dinghy from the Mount Rose snow survey rests ashore, surrounded by snow, with a snow survey crew member posing at the oars.

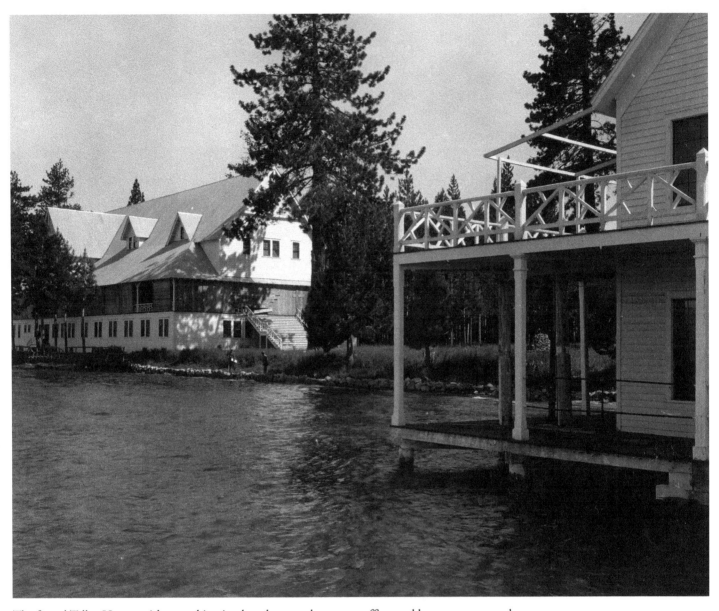

The famed Tallac House, with a combination boat house, saloon, post office, and baggage room to the right. This image is from the Lake Tahoe photographic shoreline survey of 1916-17.

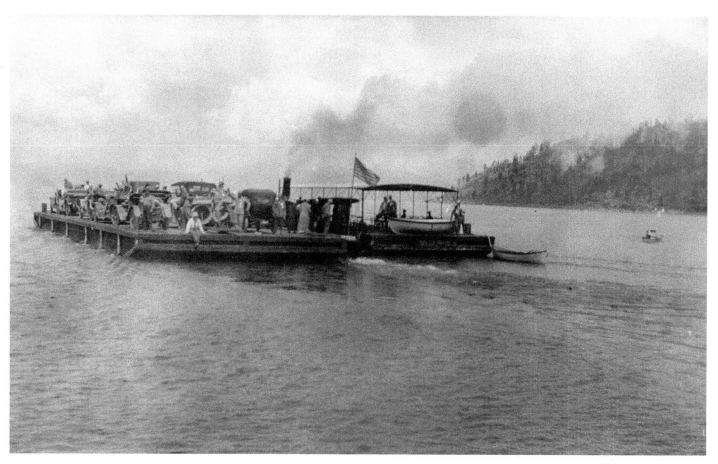

An automobile barge crosses the lake. After the logging wound down, steamships and barges once used for transporting timber carried pleasure seekers to various destinations around the lake.

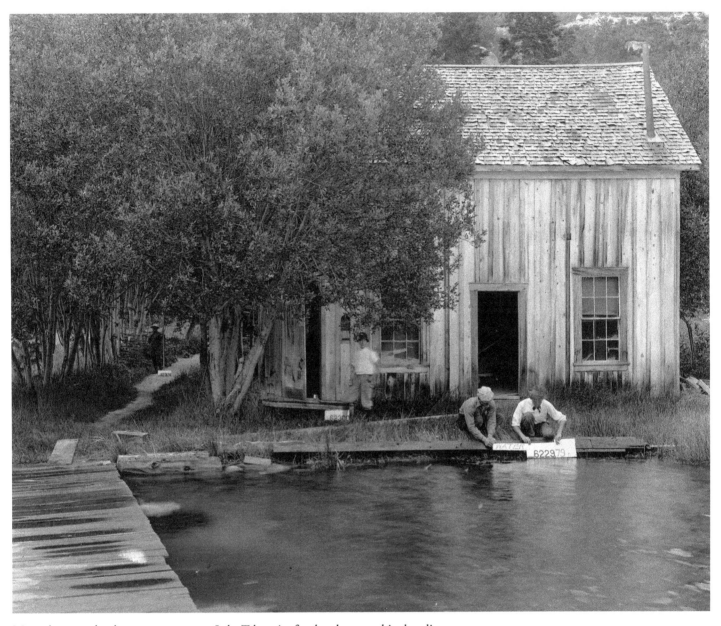

Men take water-level measurements at a Lake Tahoe site for the photographic shoreline survey commissioned by the U.S. Bureau of Reclamation.

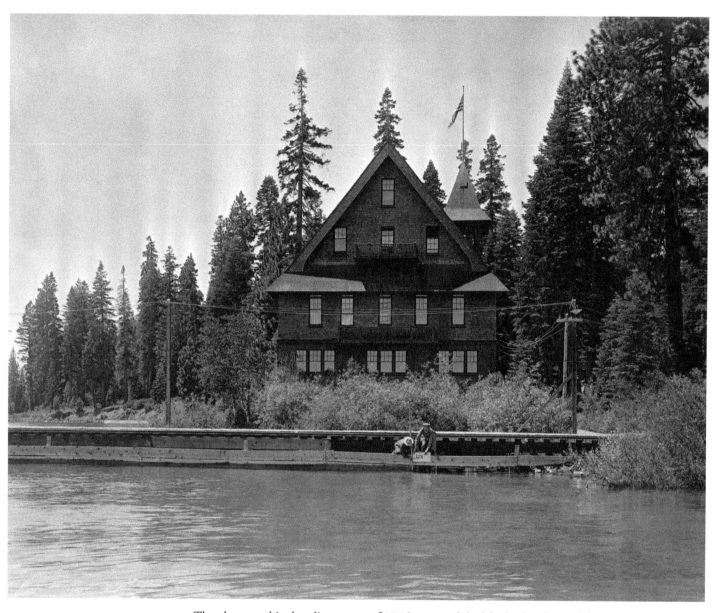

The photographic shoreline survey of 1916 measured the lake level in front of the Tahoe Tavern on the Lake Tahoe Railway and Transportation Company pier. The lake's surface was recorded at 6,231 feet above sea level.

C. O. Valentine recorded this image on August 28, 1917, at Tahoe Tavern Casino, with notes marking changes in lake level. The lake's surface was recorded at 6,229 feet above sea level, the highest for the year.

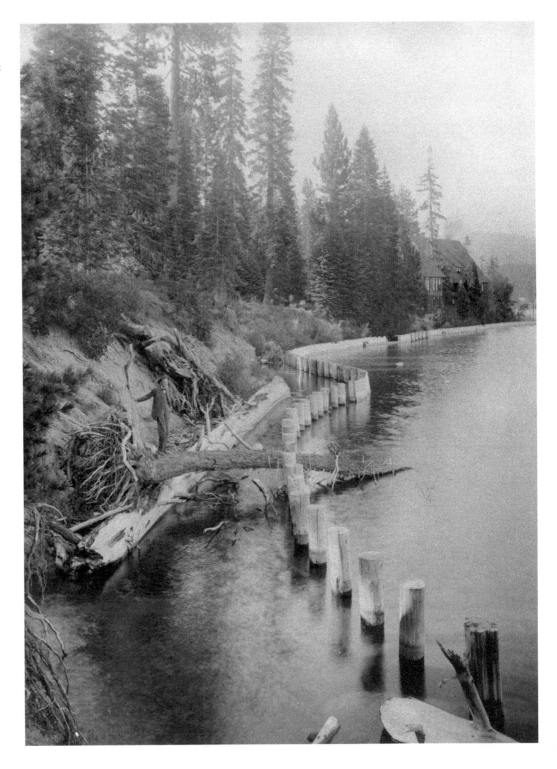

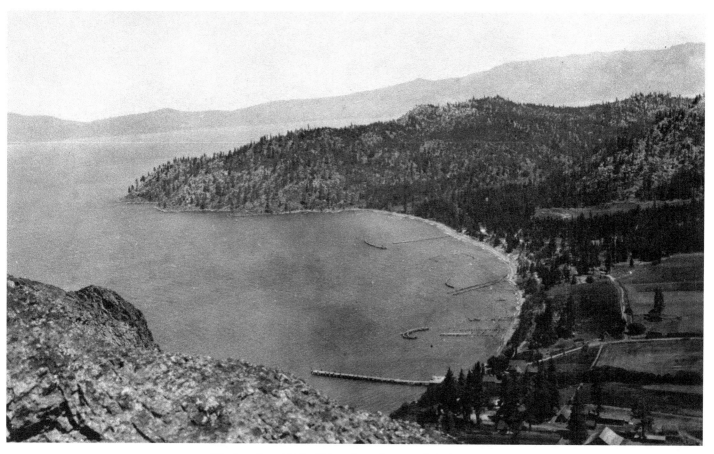

Glenbrook and Lake Tahoe from the top of Shakespeare Rock, August 3, 1919. A bird's-eye view of piers, wharves, and the vicinity reveals lingering evidence of clear-cutting of bygone years. The hillside holds little or no old-growth timber.

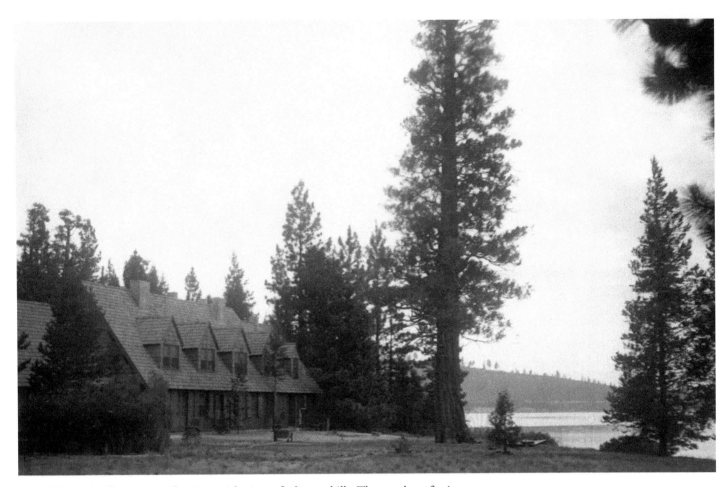

A beachfront dwelling among the pines with views of adjacent hills. The number of private summer homes and year-round residences on the lake grew steadily during the first decades of the twentieth century as the lake gained popularity.

A National Playground for All

(1921–1940)

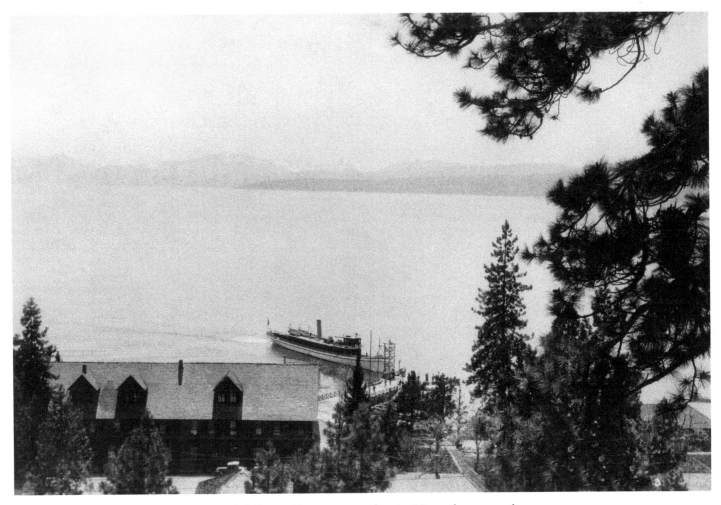

View from above the Brockway Resort at Lake Tahoe, with a steamer at the pier. No roads connected the north and south on the east side of the lake until the second decade of the 1900s, leaving visitors reliant on water transportation. In August 1925, the last section of a highway was completed connecting Glenbrook and Brockway.

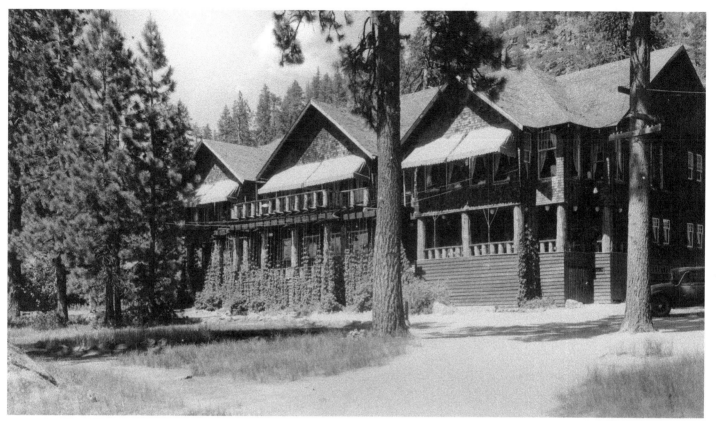

Front view of the Brockway Hotel at Brockway, California, as it appeared around the 1920s. The Brockway was built in 1917 on the site of the old Warm Springs Hotel, a health spa that included a 20-foot bathhouse built over natural, warm mineral springs. In 1924, a golf course was added to the area, which today is known as King's Beach.

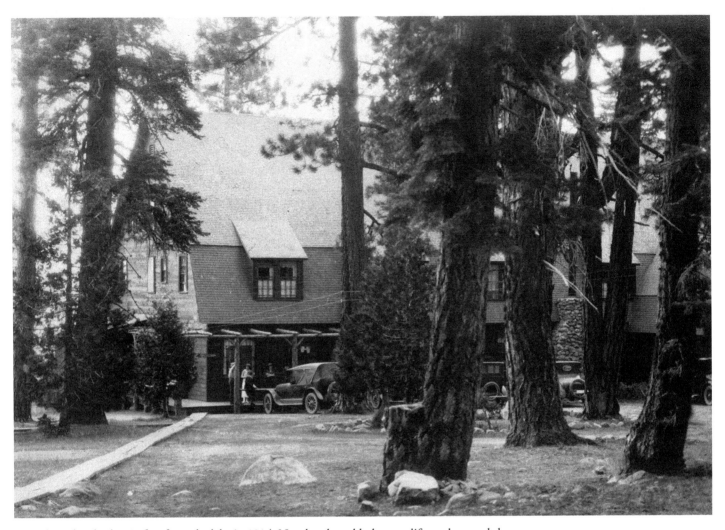

Pomin's Lodge, built 150 feet from the lake in 1914. New hotels and lodges proliferated around the lake after the turn of the century.

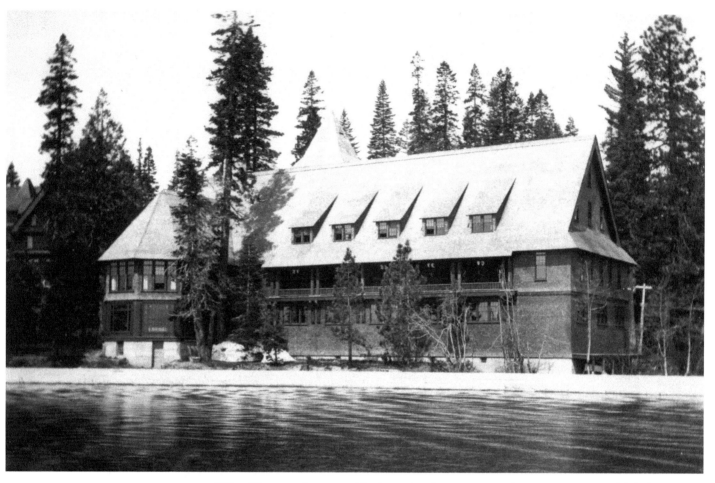

Tahoe Tavern, as it appeared in the 1920s. In 1925, a new $250,000 wing was added along with a bar, coffee shop, sun deck, movie theater, and pleasure pier. Garages for the new wave of automobile travelers were added in 1927, along with tennis courts and a livery stable.

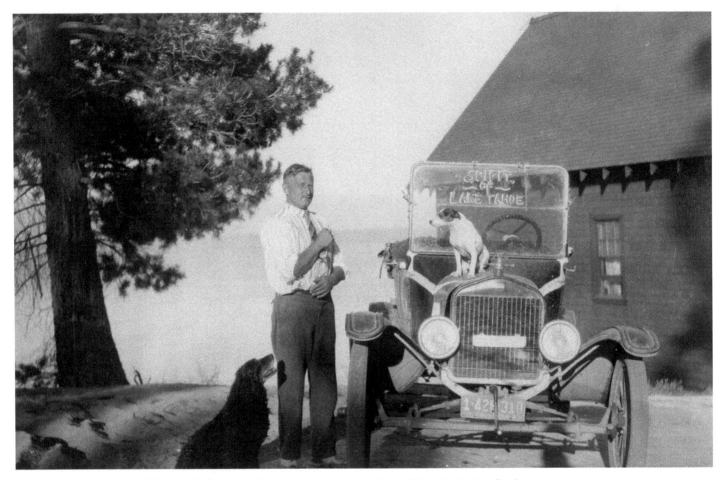

Hans Hansen, caretaker of the Newhall estate, with dogs and an automobile dubbed the *Spirit of Lake Tahoe* in 1927. Lake Tahoe attracted wealthy families from San Francisco, who built elaborate summer mansions on the lake's shores, such as the sprawling estate built for the George Newhall family in 1922.

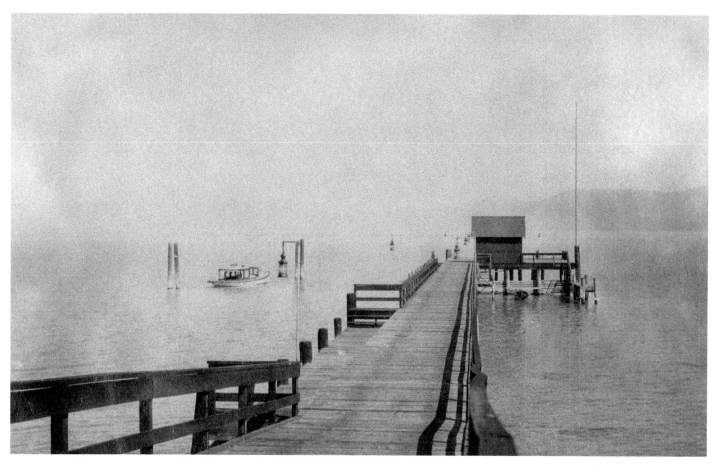

A small boat and the pier at the Newhall estate in 1926. In addition to their large estate at Rubicon Bay, the family purchased a second property at Skunk Harbor on the eastern shore of Tahoe, so that they and friends would have a boating destination.

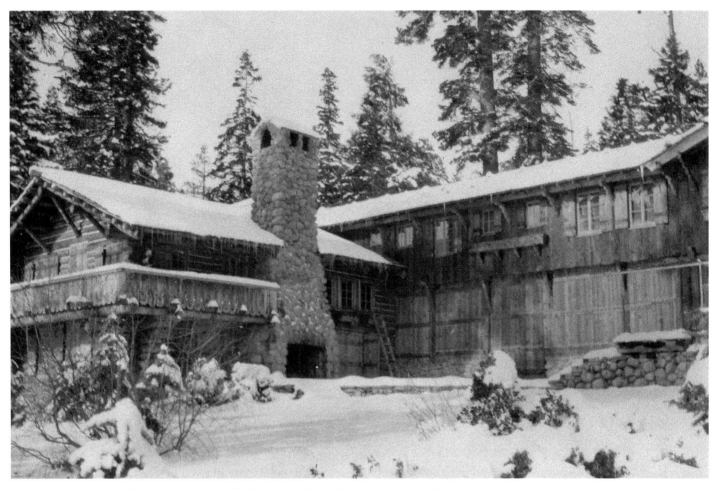

A 1927 winter view of the Drum estate at Lake Tahoe. Hollywood movies set in northern climes were often filmed in Tahoe. The first, *Indian Love Call*, starring Jeanette MacDonald and Nelson Eddy, was set in the Rockies and featured a Canadian Mountie love interest.

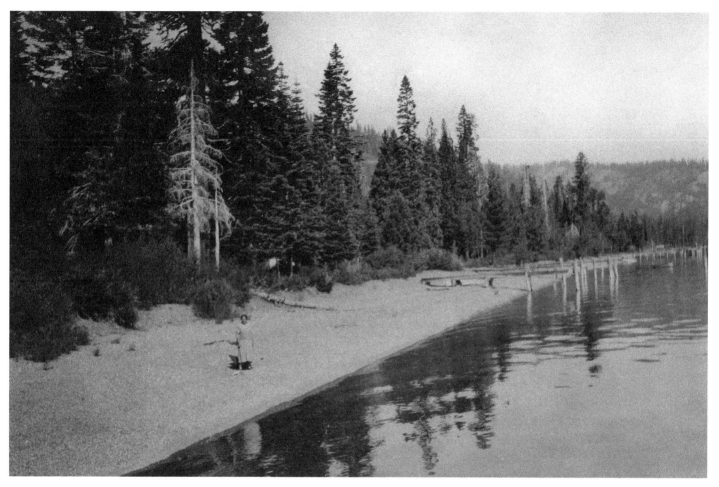

The Rubicon Lodge beach.

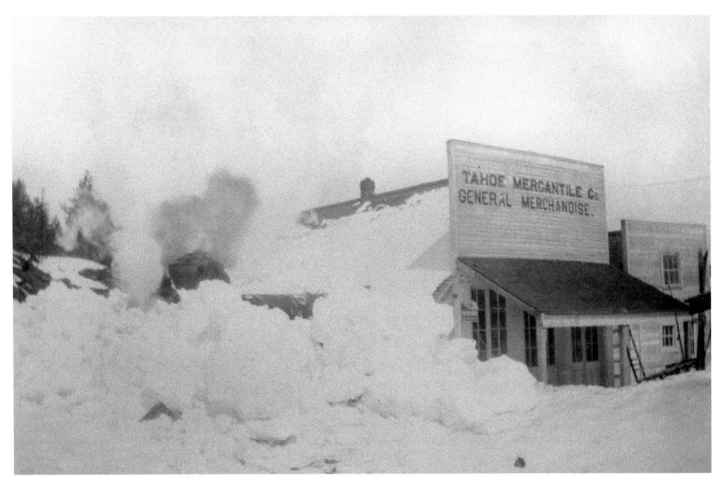

Winter view of the Tahoe Mercantile Company in Tahoe City.

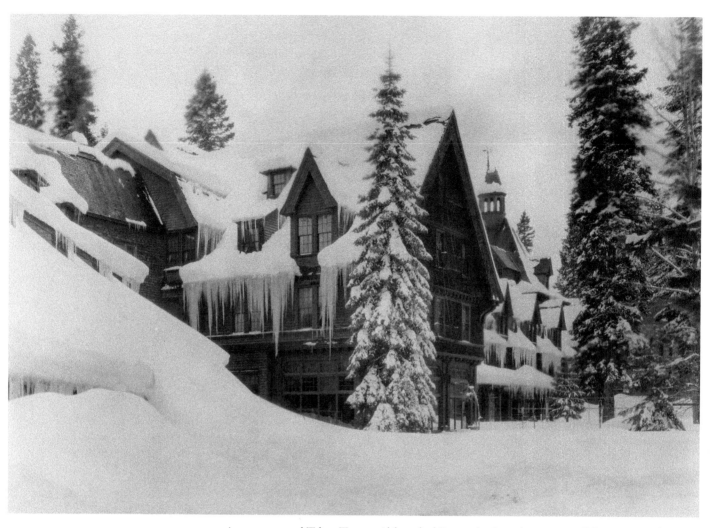

A snow-covered Tahoe Tavern. Although skiing and other winter sports did not gain widespread popularity in the basin until after World War II, the Tahoe City Ski Club constructed a ski jump south of town in the 1920s. This area, known as Granlibakken, was the site of U.S. Olympic Committee trials for the 1932 Olympics.

In 1931, a tunnel was blasted through Cave Rock as part of a new highway. The Kingsbury Grade, Spooner Summit, and the Mount Rose highway were all built during the 1920s and 1930s, replacing older, unpaved routes and making visits to the lake easier and more convenient year-round.

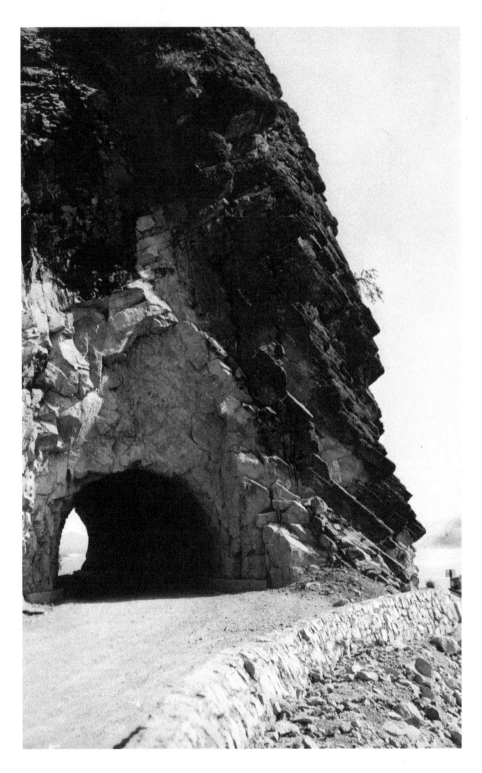

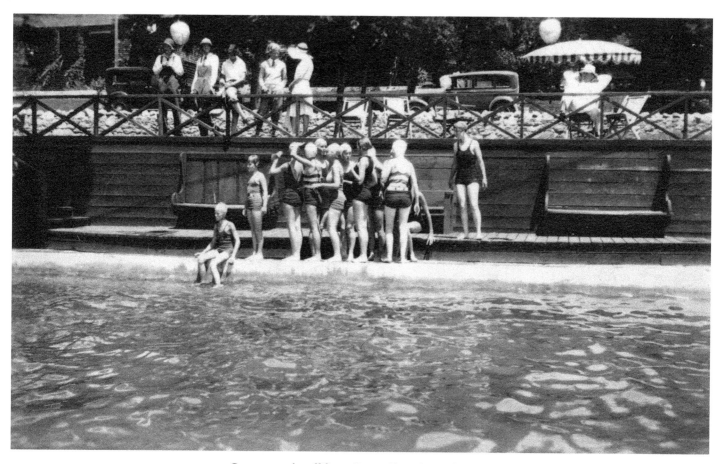

Campers and staff from Camp Chonokis at the Brockway, California, swimming pool. Founders Mabel Winter and Ethel Pope believed that girls could benefit from a loosely structured outdoor experience after the more regimented program of their schools. The regular camp session lasted six weeks.

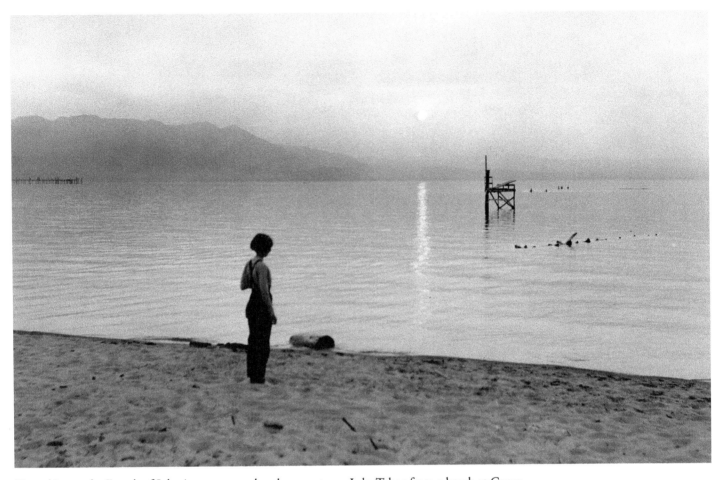

Hazy skies on the Fourth of July. A camper watches the sunset over Lake Tahoe from a beach at Camp Chonokis.

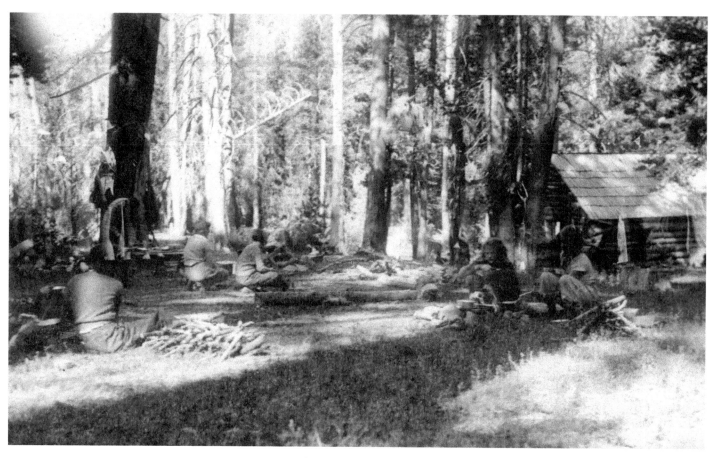

Camp Chonokis campers prepare a campfire meal at Armstrong's at Emerald Bay.

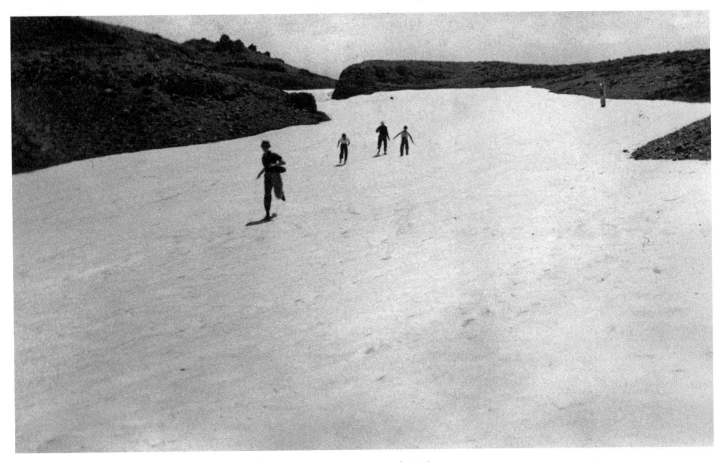

Camp Chonokis girls play on a field of snow at Carson Pass in the summer of 1934.

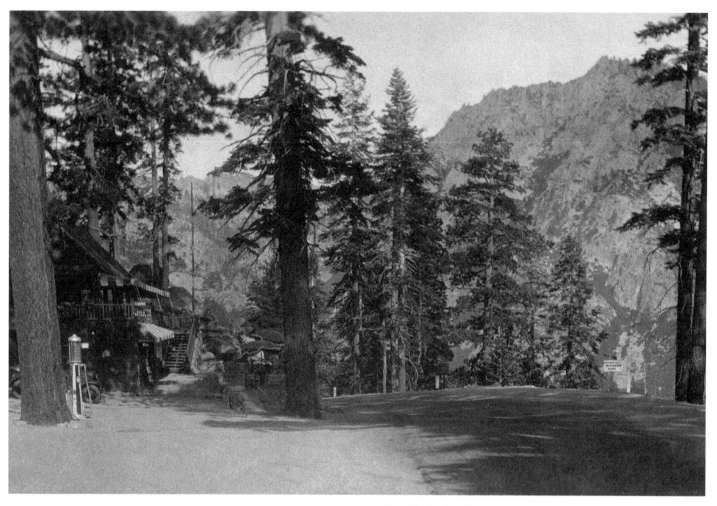

Outside the Bay View Resort near Inspiration Point, Lake Tahoe.

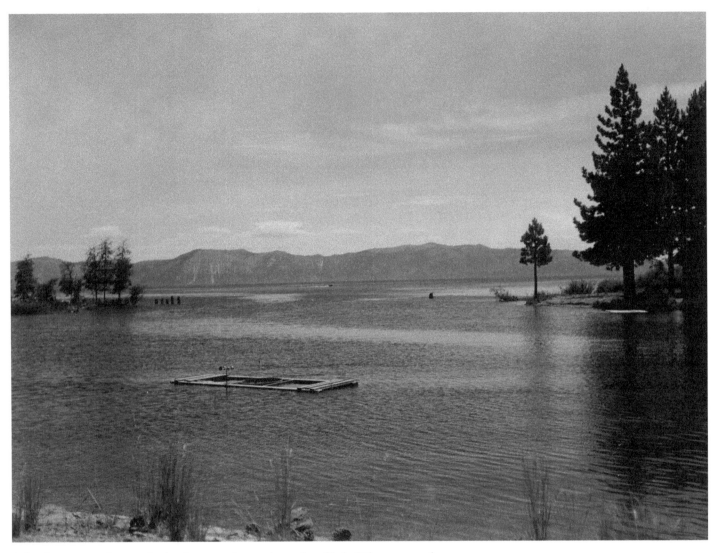

A floating evaporation pan in the river mouth near the outlet of Lake Tahoe was used to measure evaporation from the lake's surface.

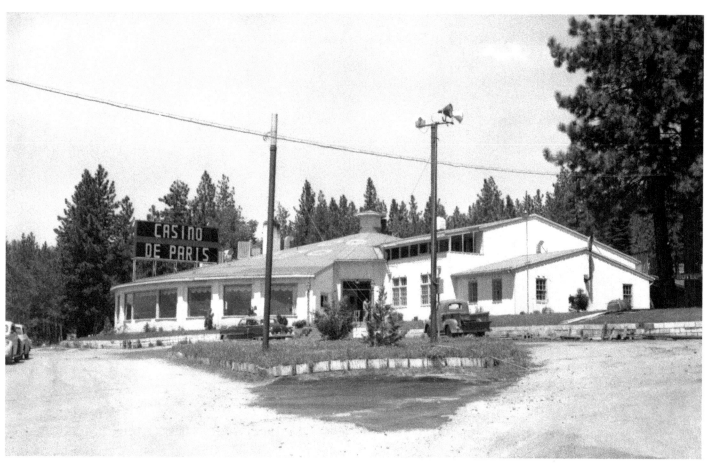

Outside the Casino de Paris, on the Nevada side of the lake. In 1931, the Nevada legislature lifted a ban on gambling, which had been set in place in 1910 (though often ignored). Gamblers from California flocked across the state line and casinos began to spring up on the Nevada shores.

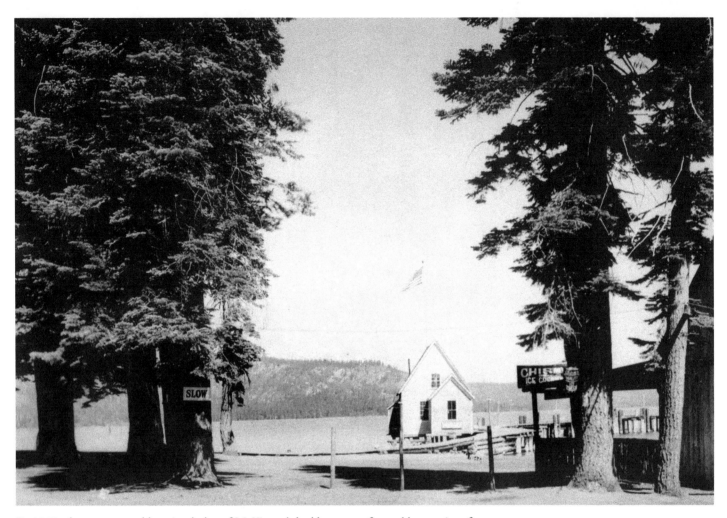

By 1920, the once rugged hunting lodge of McKinney's had been transformed by a series of new owners into a modern hotel that could accommodate 200 visitors.

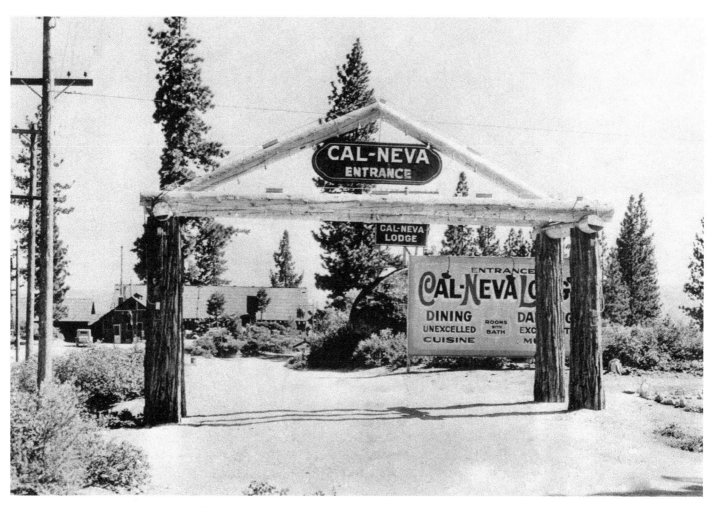

Signs at the entrance to the Cal-Neva Lodge with the lodge in the background. The original Cal-Neva Lake Tahoe Resort Spa Casino quickly became a playground for celebrities and socialites who wanted to escape the public eye.

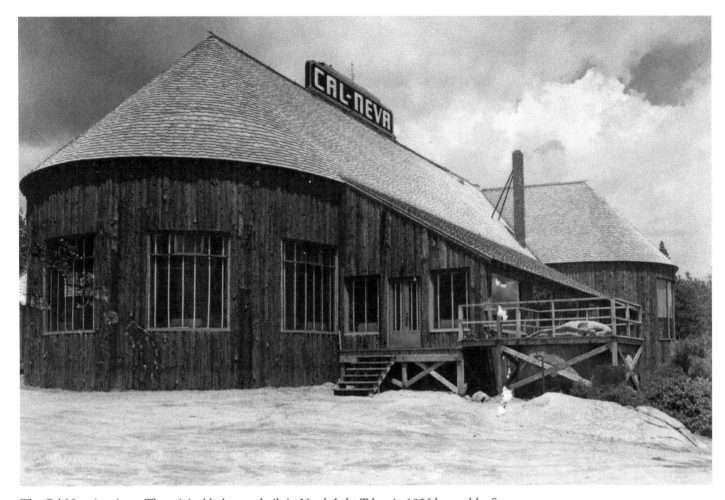

The Cal-Neva in winter. The original lodge was built in North Lake Tahoe in 1926 by wealthy San Francisco businessman Robert P. Sherman, who used it as a guest house for his friends and real estate clients. It was modeled on Frank Bacon's log cabin in the hit Broadway play *Lightnin'*, set on the California-Nevada state line where would-be divorcees check in. Will Rogers starred in the 1930 film version.

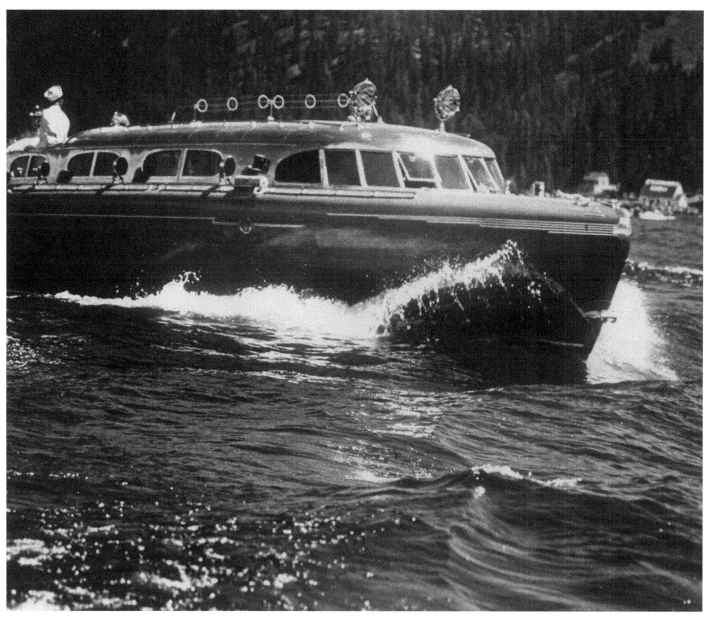

The *Thunderbird*, a motorboat belonging to George Whittell, Jr., on Lake Tahoe.

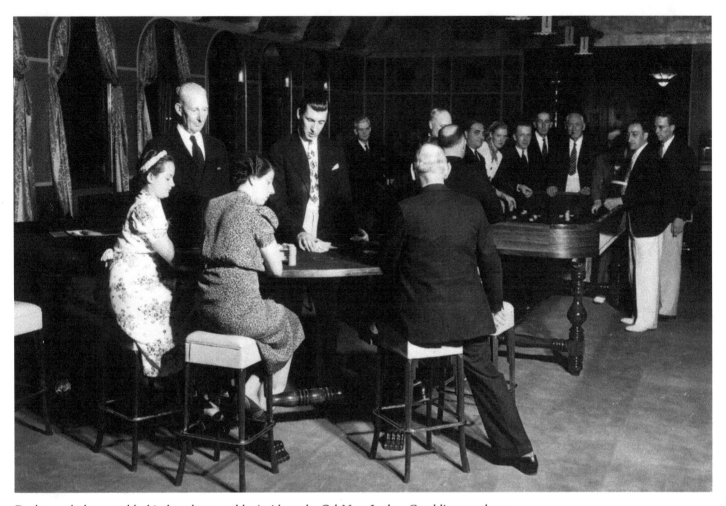

Dealers and players at blackjack and craps tables inside at the Cal-Neva Lodge. Gambling caught on slowly after its legalization in the midst of the Great Depression; most casinos were open only during the summer.

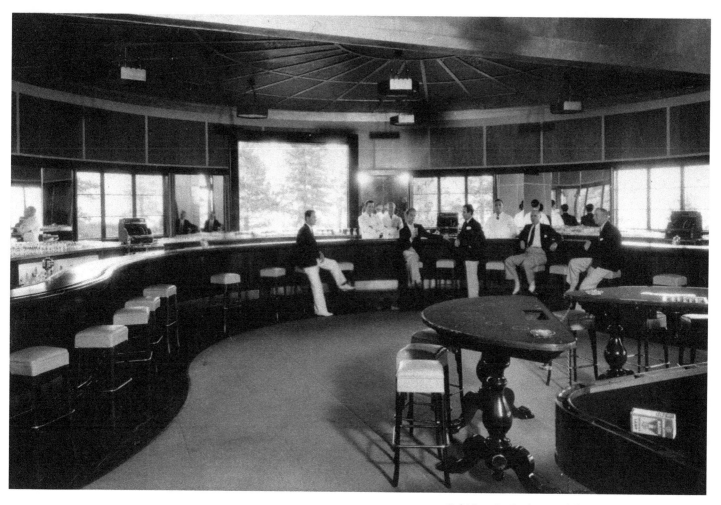

Cal-Neva Lodge bar, with bartenders and customers.

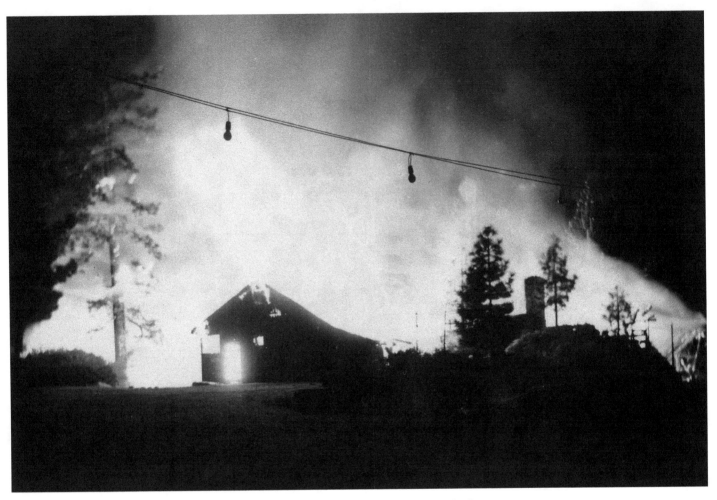

The Cal-Neva Lodge at Lake Tahoe as it burns to the ground on May 17, 1937. It was rebuilt in just over 30 days by Norman Biltz and Adler Larson, early North Lake Tahoe pioneers and developers. To complete the new building, 500 men were employed around the clock.

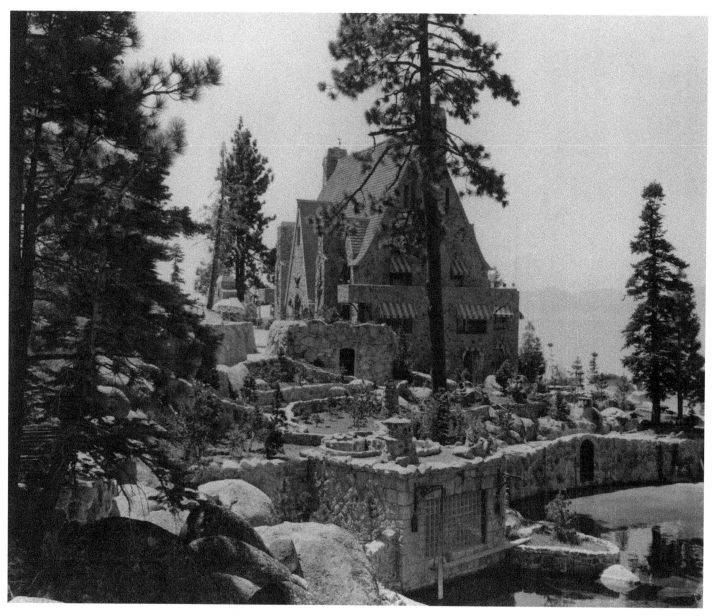

Thunderbird Lodge, the main house on the George Whittell, Jr., estate. In 1938, San Francisco millionaire Whittell bought over 24,000 acres of lakefront and backcountry forest land—most of the Nevada side of the lake—and commissioned prominent Reno architect Frederic DeLongchamps to design a mansion. The estate featured a six-hundred-foot tunnel connecting the mansion with the boat house where Whittell berthed his 55-foot mahogany yacht, *Thunderbird*.

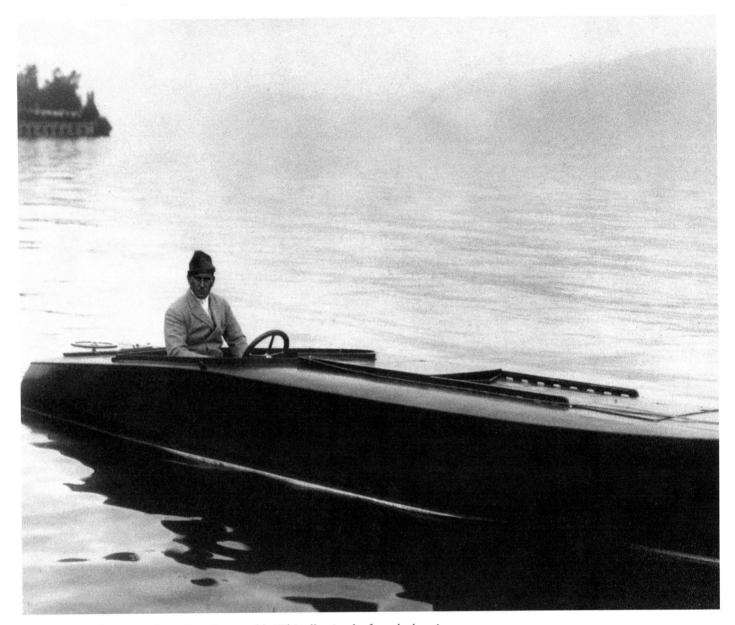

George Whittell in a speedboat. Born into wealth, Whittell resisted a formal education as a teenager, choosing instead to travel with the Barnum and Bailey Circus. During World War I, he served as an ambulance driver and a U.S. Army captain. Several months before Wall Street's Great Crash of 1929, Whittell liquidated $50 million in stocks and moved his fortune from California to Nevada, a state regarded as a tax haven for affluent Americans.

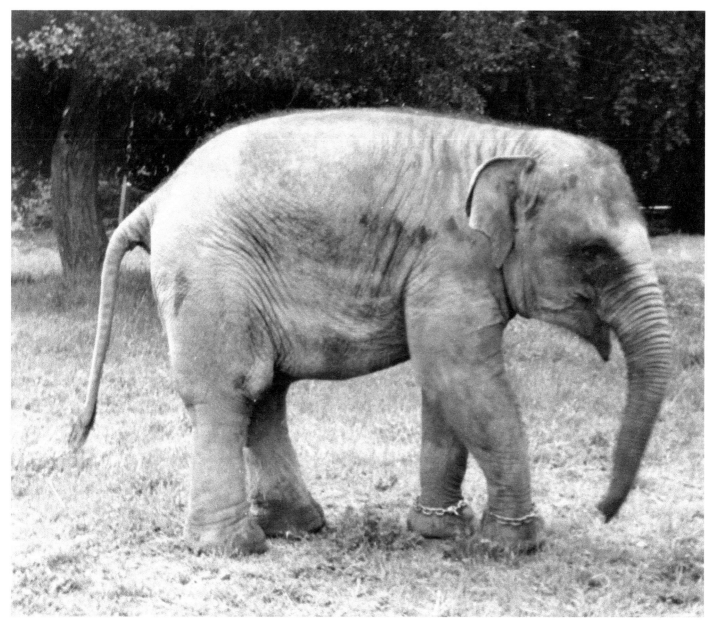

George Whittell's elephant Mingo, which he housed in a stable with lions and other exotic pets.

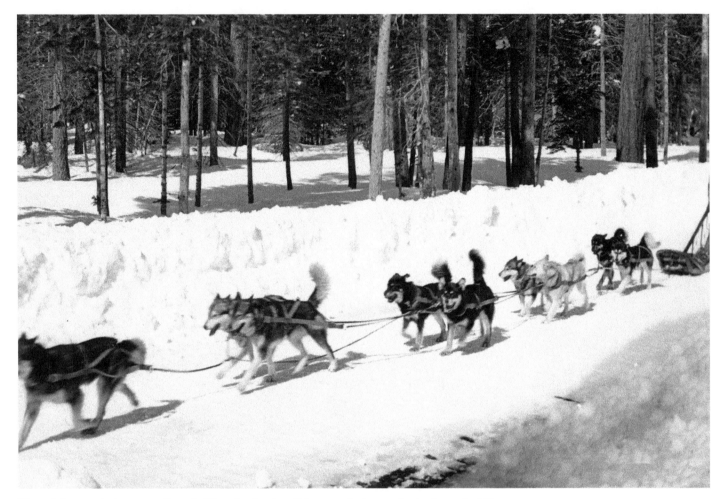

Harry Johansson's dog team. Born in Uppsala, Sweden, Johansson had extensive backwoods skills. Two months after winning U.S. citizenship in 1934, he was sworn in as Tahoe City's constable. His jurisdiction included more than 200 square miles of rugged terrain, and Harry's dogsled experience provided him access to the far-flung outposts of the district. The dogs, and Harry, had previously been celebrities in locally filmed epics such as *Call of the Wild* (in which Harry stood in for Clark Gable) and *White Fang*.

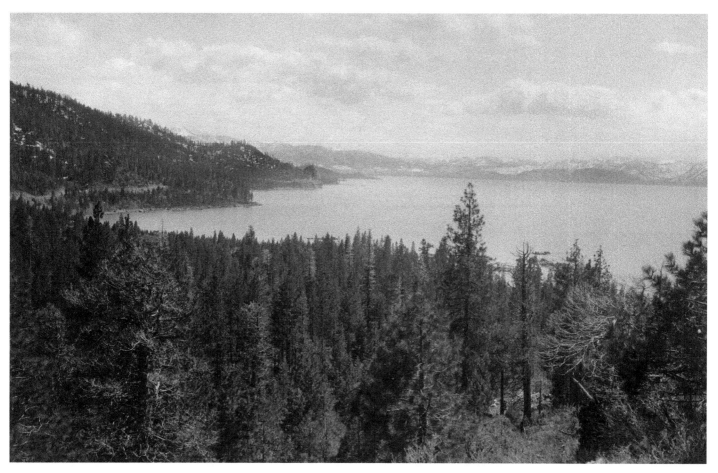
Bird's-eye view of Lake Tahoe.

The Homemakers Club at the
Skyland 4-H camp on the Nevada
side of the lake in 1938.

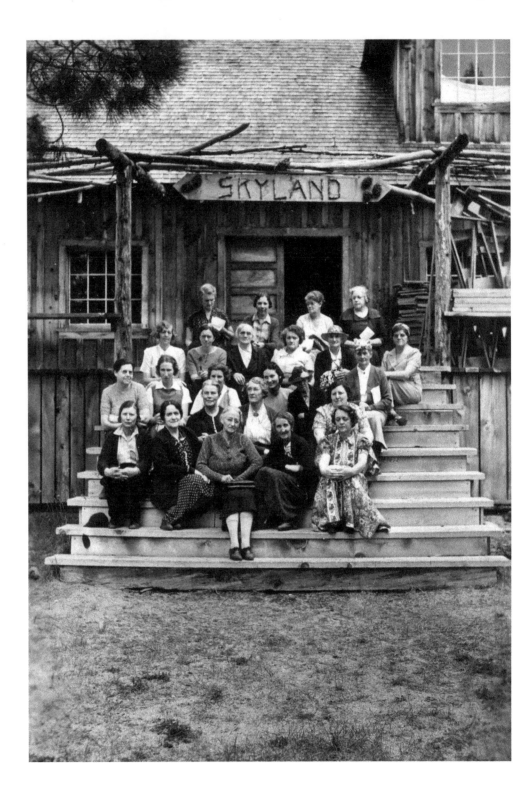

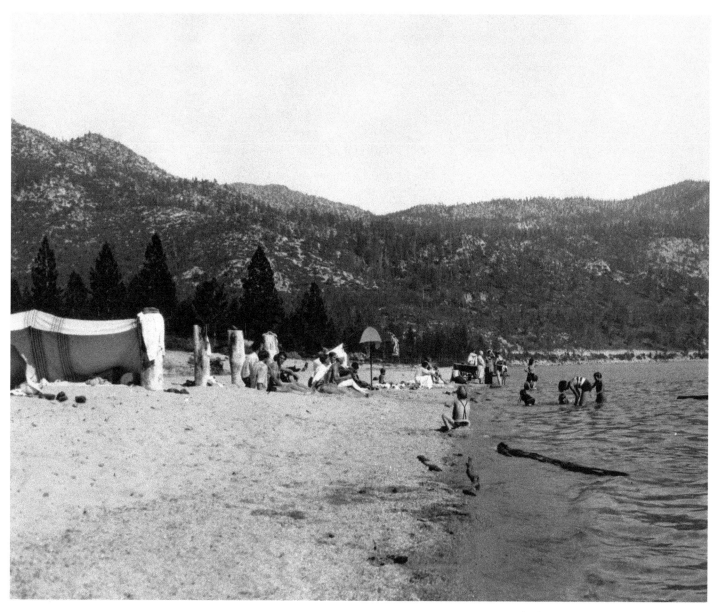

Sunbathers and waders at Incline Village.

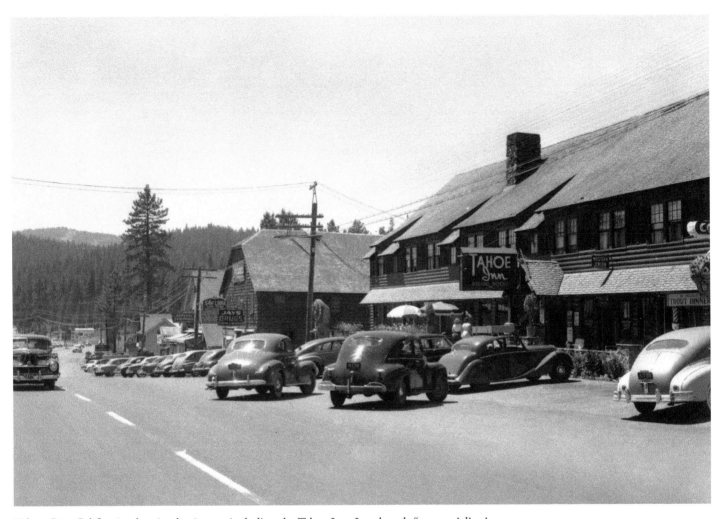

Tahoe City, California, showing businesses including the Tahoe Inn. Its ad reads "we specialize in trout dinners."

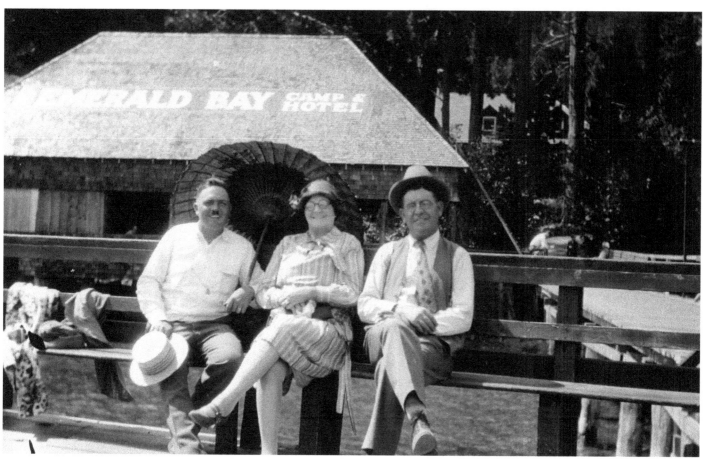

Cora and Verner Adams are among the guests at Emerald Bay Camp and Hotel on this day at the lake. The bay, a favored destination for boats, was home to many comfortable family resorts.

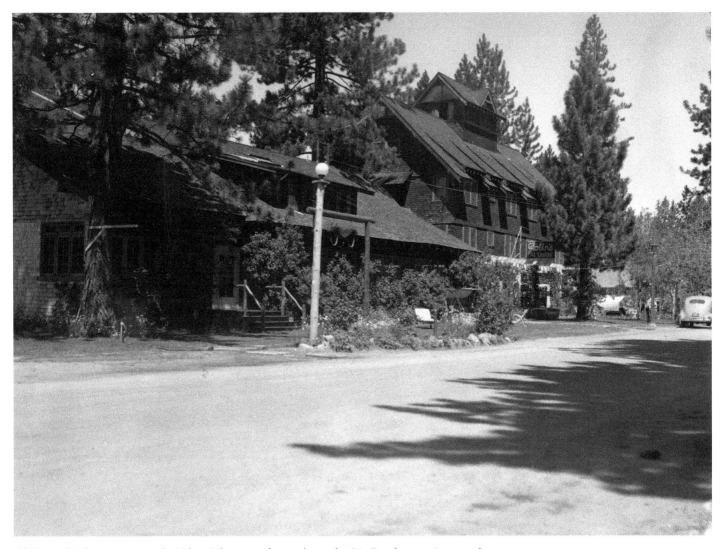

Globin's Al Tahoe resort at Lake Tahoe. The resort featured popular Big Band entertainers such as Count Basie, Glen Miller, and the Dorseys.

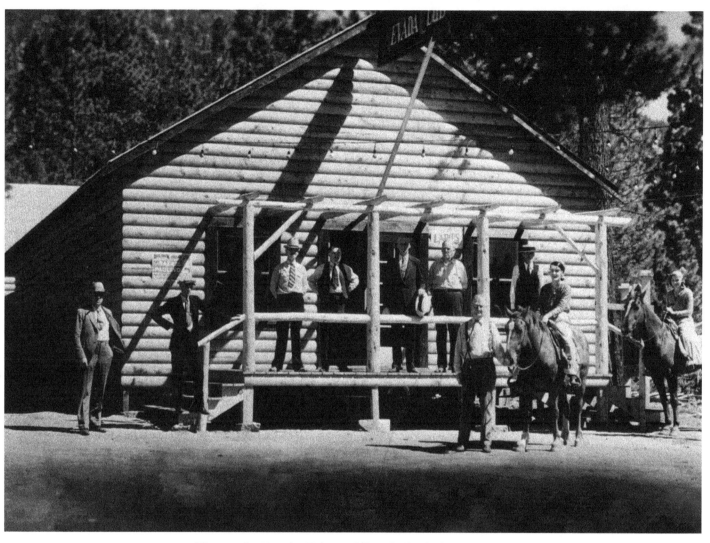

The popular Nevada Club, straddling the border between California and Nevada, would later become Harrah's Lake Club and then Harveys Lake Tahoe.

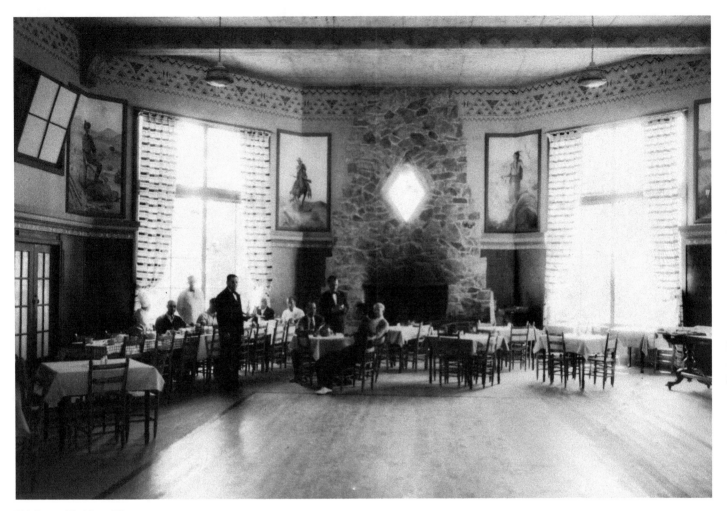

Dining at Ta-Neva-Ho.

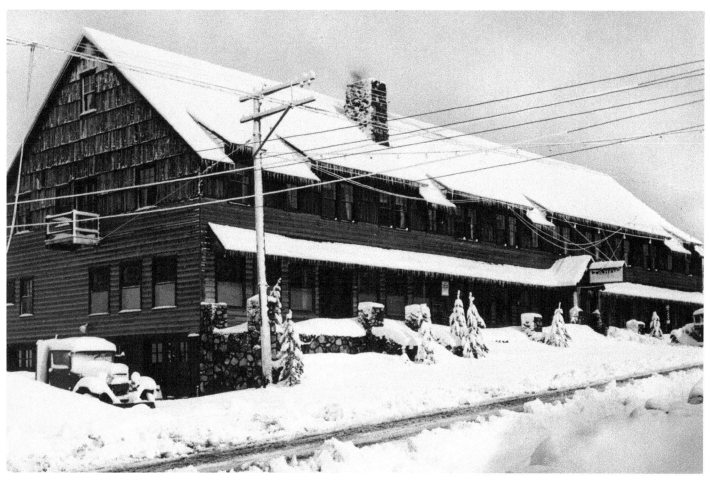

The Tahoe Inn was sold to the Bechdolt family in 1923 and rebuilt after burning to the ground in 1934. The inn was used as a speakeasy during Prohibition and was said to be a favorite of infamous guests such as gangster "Baby-Face" Nelson.

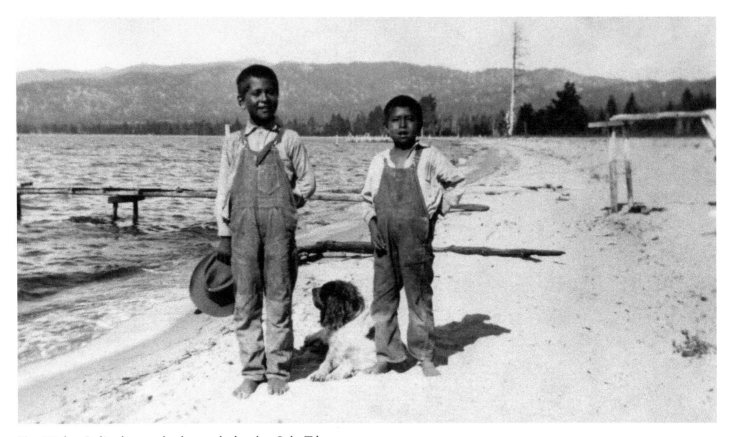

Two Washoe Indian boys and a dog on the beach at Lake Tahoe.

CLAIM TO FAME

(1941–1960s)

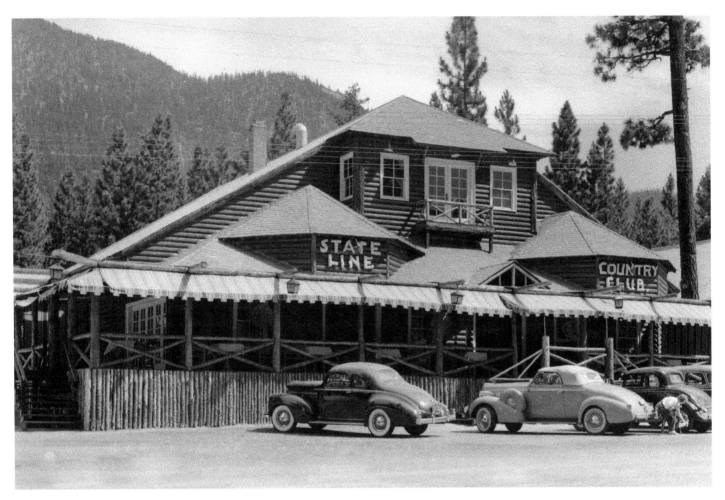

The State Line Country Club casino in the early 1940s.

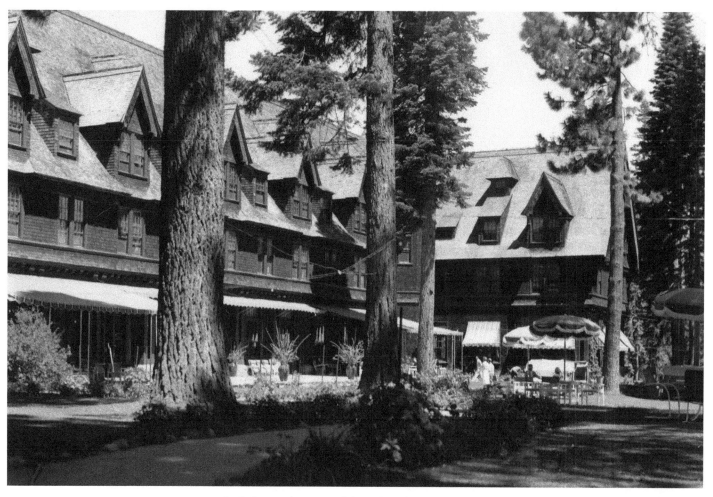

An infamous hangout of the rich and near-great in the early 1900s, the Tahoe Tavern was the last word in luxury, housing a casino, stage, ballroom, bowling alley, barber shop, and retail shops for its clientele.

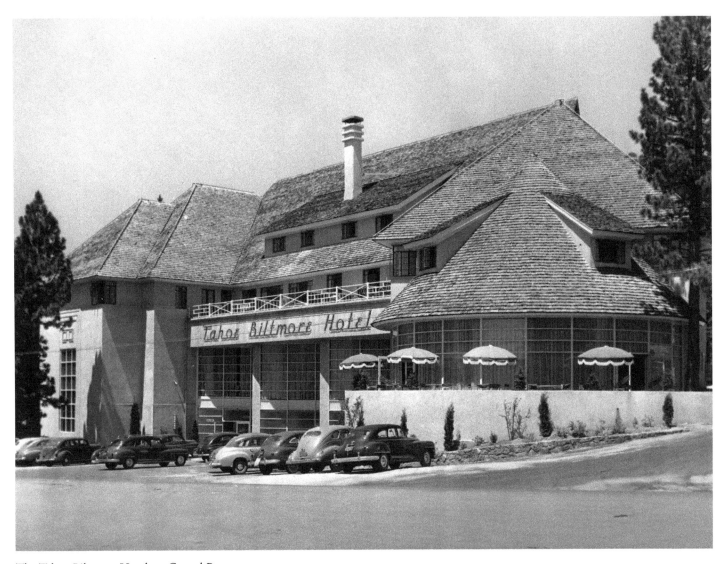

The Tahoe Biltmore Hotel on Crystal Bay.

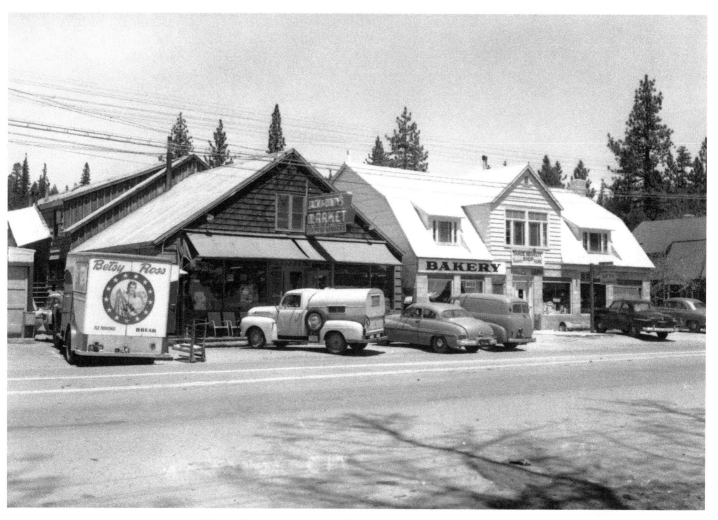

Tahoe City in the 1940s. Before the highway system, the town was best reached by the narrow-gauge railroad connecting the town to the Southern Pacific Railroad in Truckee. The emergence of tourism by automobile drastically altered the local economy—one casualty was the Tahoe Tavern, lost when its real estate went for other purposes.

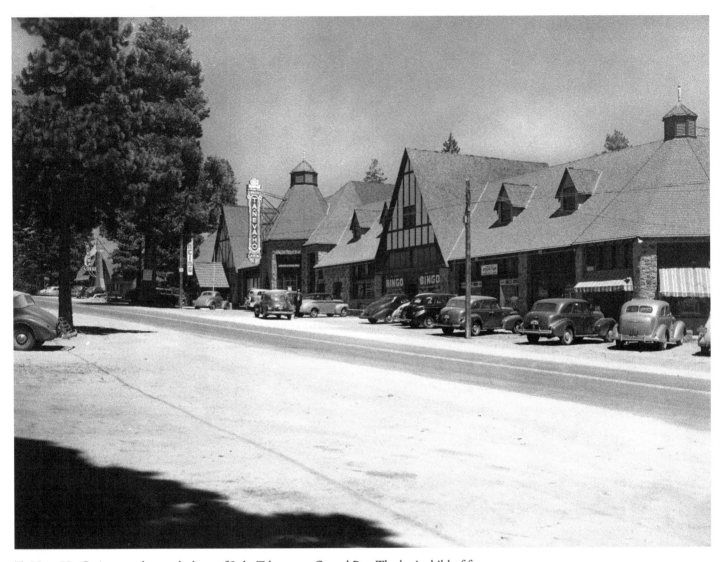

Ta-Neva-Ho Casino, on the north shore of Lake Tahoe near Crystal Bay. The brainchild of former Buckhorn restaurant owner Johnny Rayburn, the Ta-Neva-Ho housed a bowling alley and the Bucket of Blood Saloon.

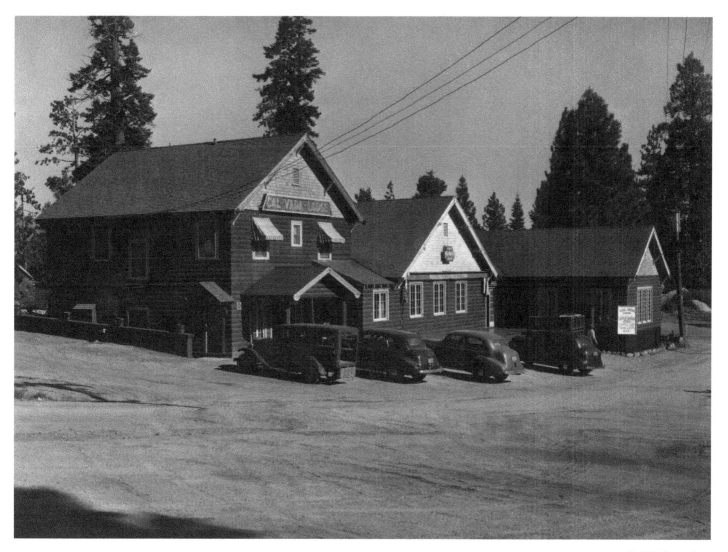

Cal-Vada Lodge.

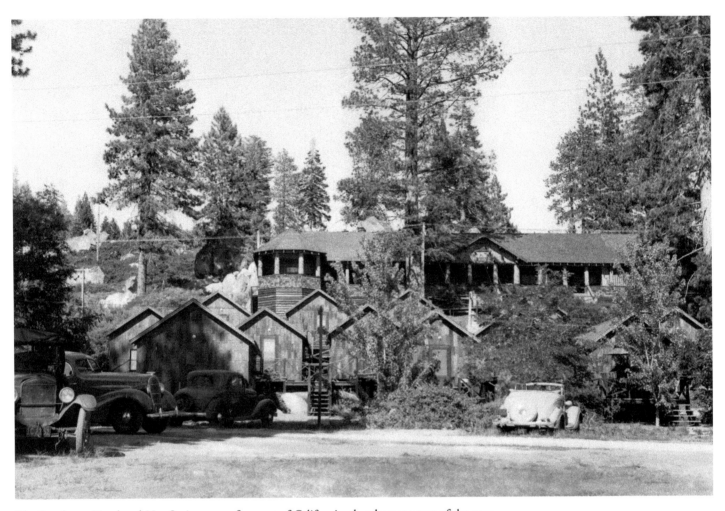

The Brockway Hotel and Hot Springs were first part of California, then became part of the new state of Nevada, and were finally returned to California as state boundaries were revised. In 1973, the former hotel's rooms began to be sold as "timeshares," the first time the term was used to describe an interval of vacation time purchased from a resort.

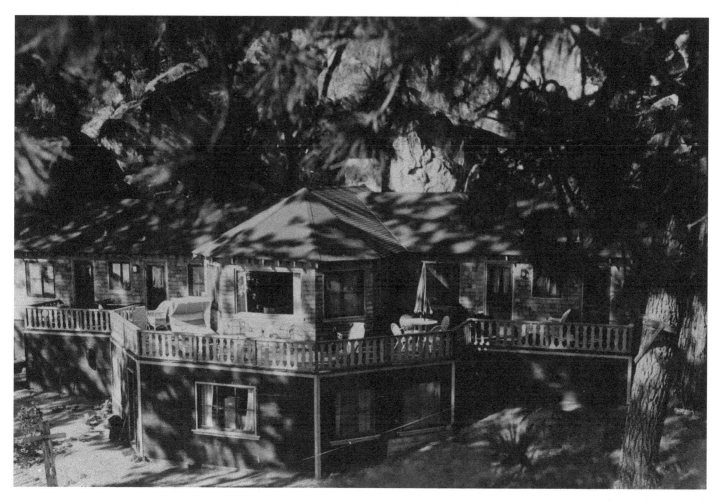

A cottage at the Brockway Hotel.

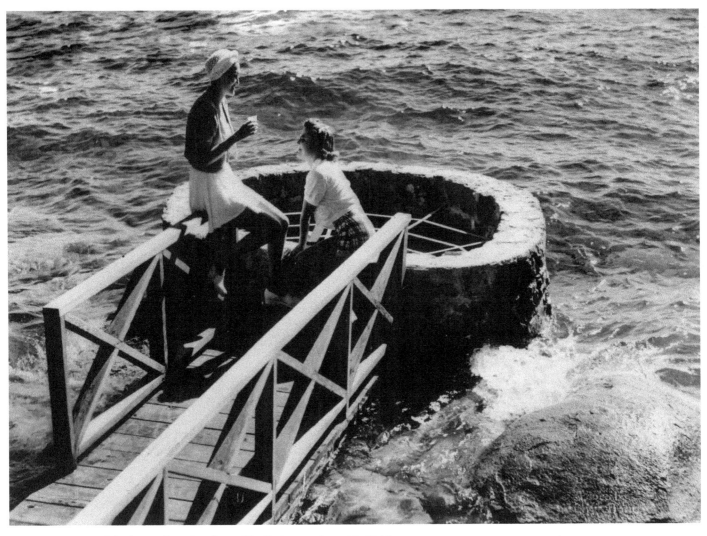

Guests enjoy one of the hot wells at Brockway Hot Springs on June 12, 1946.

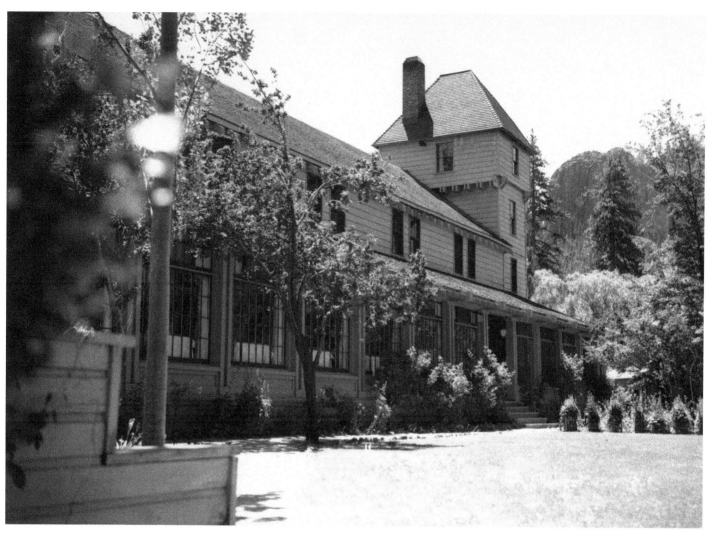

The Glenbrook Inn. By the 1940s, the era of gilded luxury resorts like the Glenbrook was nearing its end. Such storied properties gave way to towering gambling palaces as the century unfolded.

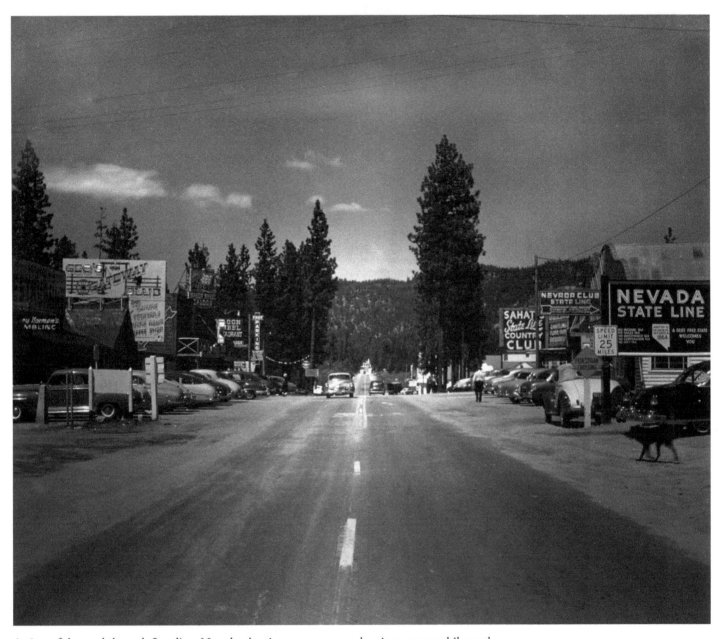

A view of the road through Stateline, Nevada, showing restaurants and casinos, automobiles and pedestrians. The emergence of year-round tourism at the lake drove economic development and added permanent residents to lakeside communities.

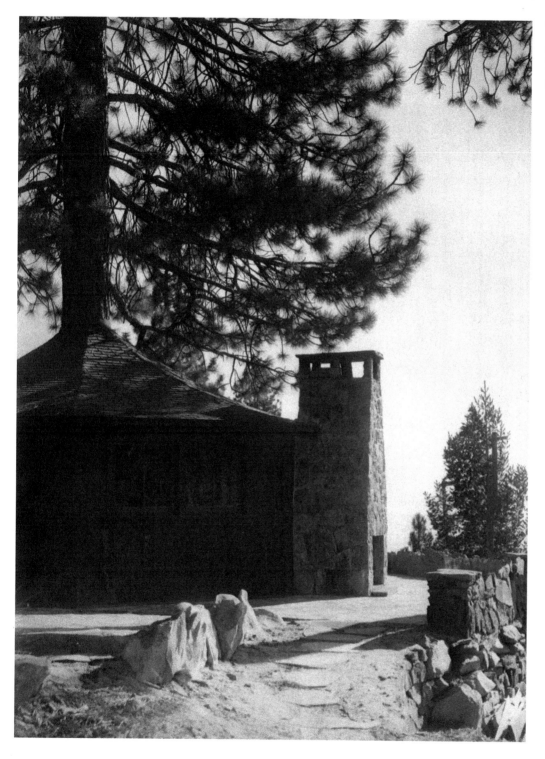

The "tree house" of Dr. James A. Church of the University of Nevada, the father of the snow surveys in the Tahoe area.

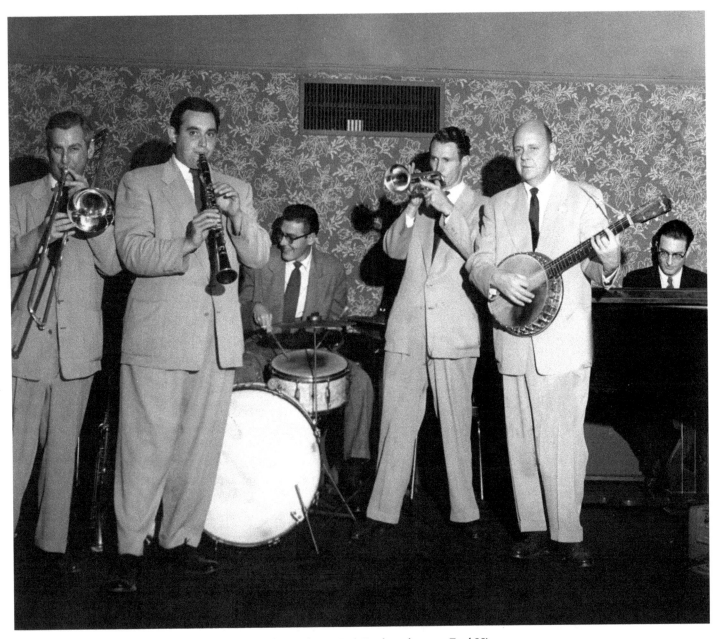

Scobey's Frisco Band performs on July 25, 1953. Left to right are Jack Buck, unknown, Fred Higuera, Bob Scobey, Clancy Hayes, Burt Bales.

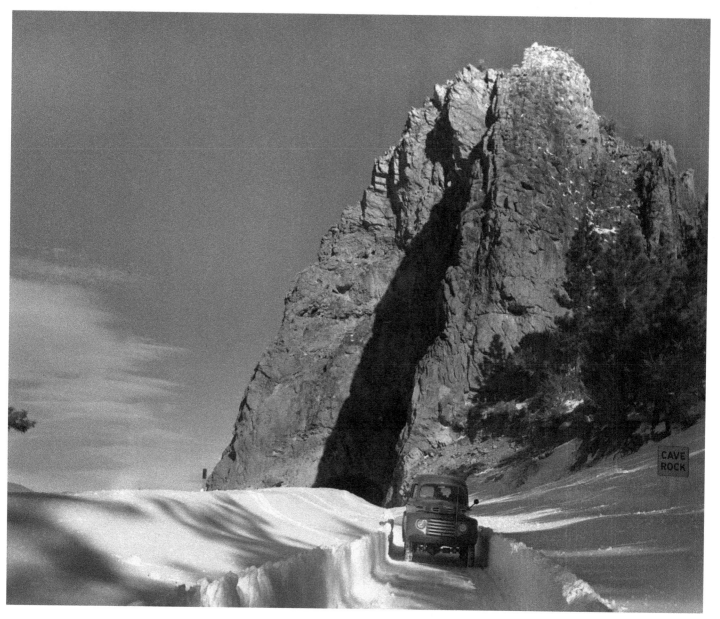

CAVE
ROCK

The Cave Rock tunnel road as it looked one winter in the 1950s.

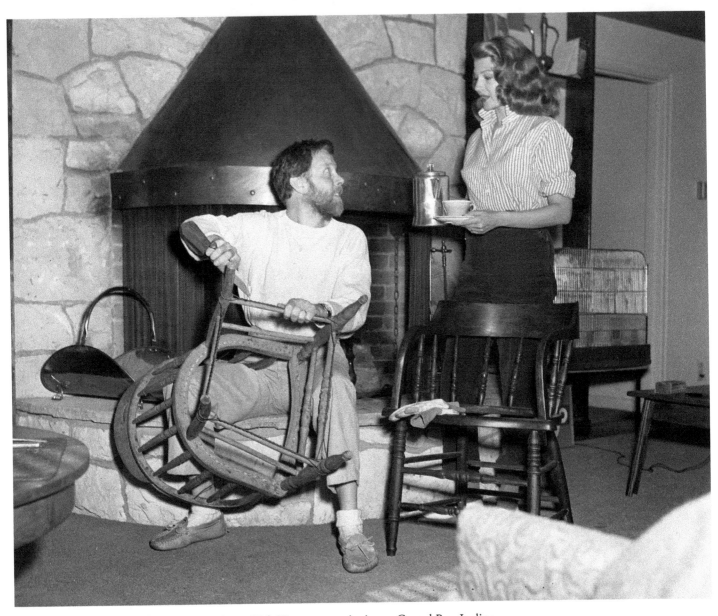

Actress Rita Hayworth and Argentinean singer Dick Haymes, vacationing at Crystal Bay, Incline Beach.

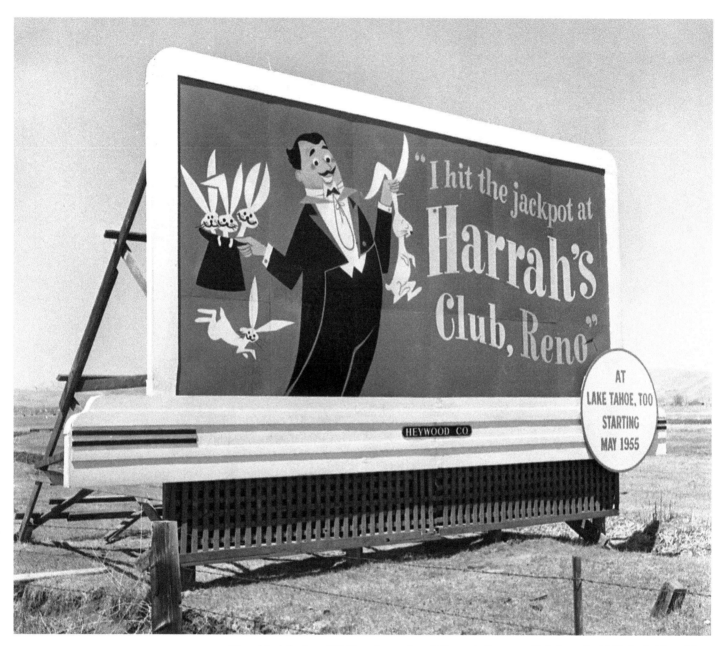

Harrah's club sign. Bill Harrah purchased George's Gateway Club in early 1955 for half a million dollars and reopened it as Harrah's Lake Club five months later. In 1958, Harrah bought the Stateline Country Club and the Nevada Club on the other side of the street and built the Harrah's Stateline Club.

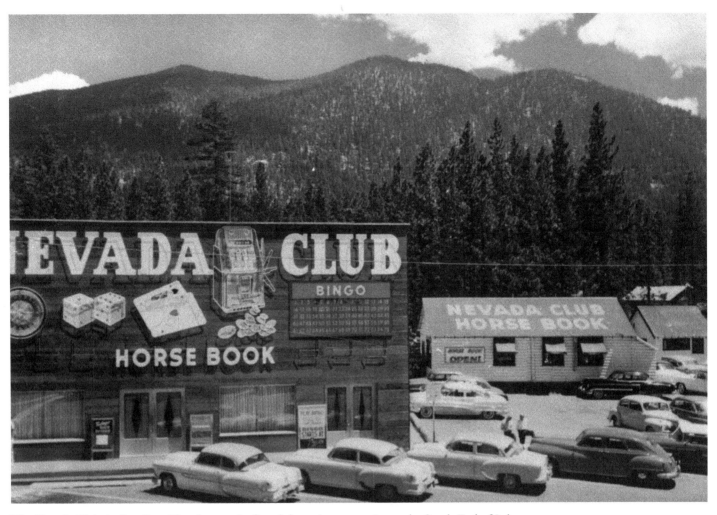

The Nevada Club, in Stateline, Nevada, was the first club to pioneer gaming at the South End of Lake Tahoe. It was owned and operated by Clyde Beecher and Bud Beecher.

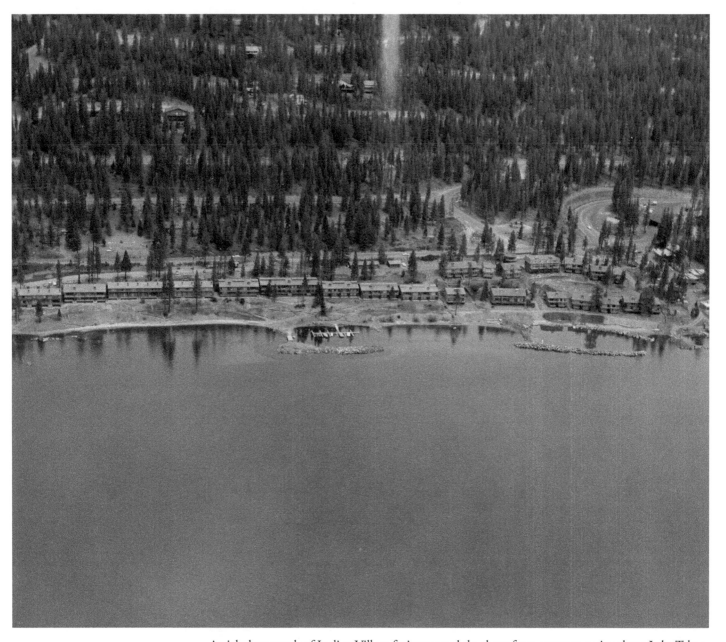

Aerial photograph of Incline Village facing toward the shore from a vantage point above Lake Tahoe. This image comes from the Lake Tahoe Area Council photograph collection.

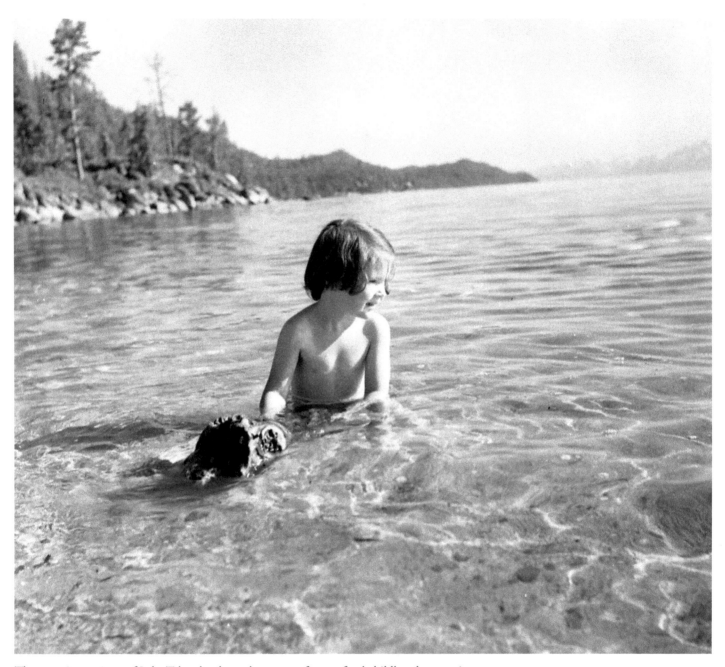

The stunning majesty of Lake Tahoe has been the source of many fond childhood memories.

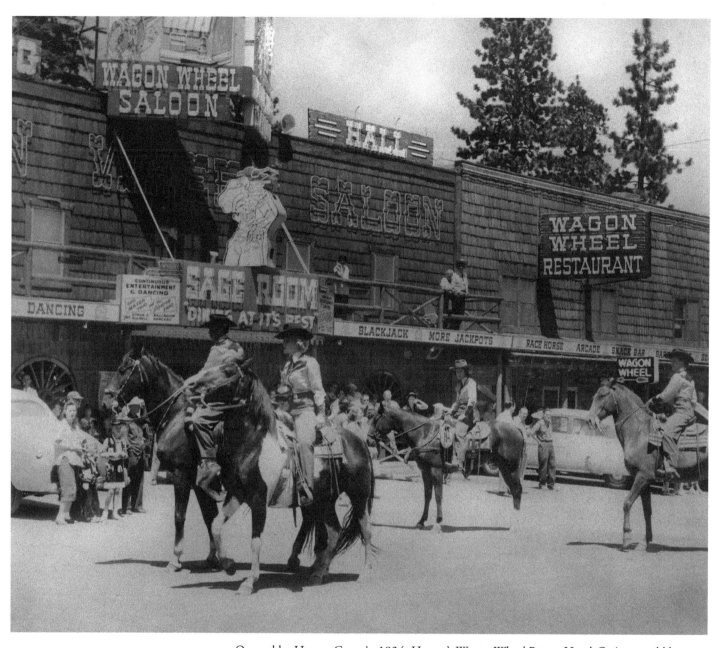

Opened by Harvey Gross in 1934, Harvey's Wagon Wheel Resort Hotel-Casino would become the first casino with a wooden boardwalk and would lay claim in the 1950s to having the most slot machines under one roof. In the foreground, Harvey's wife Llewellyn Gross, and daughter, Beverlee G. Ledbetter, take part in a Western Days celebration.

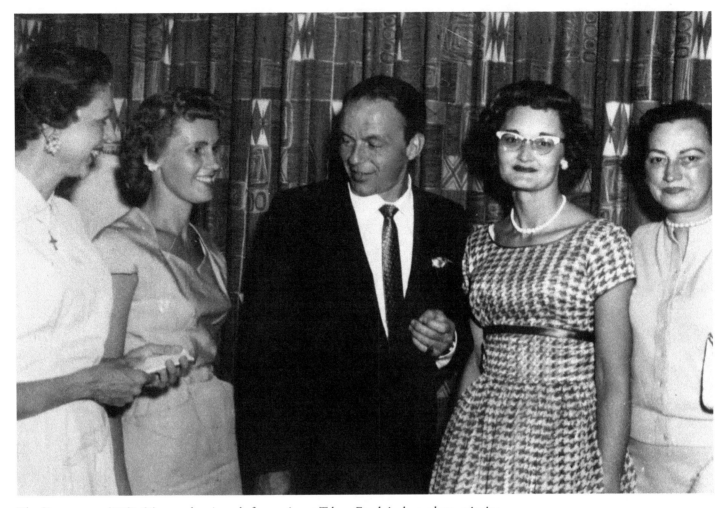

The Sinatra years (1960-63) were the pinnacle for gaming at Tahoe. Frank is shown here enjoying the company of locals backstage. Left to right are Ceta Hooper, Mrs. Tom Hoffman, Frank Sinatra, Harriet Price, and Bethel Van Tassel at the Cal-Neva Lodge.

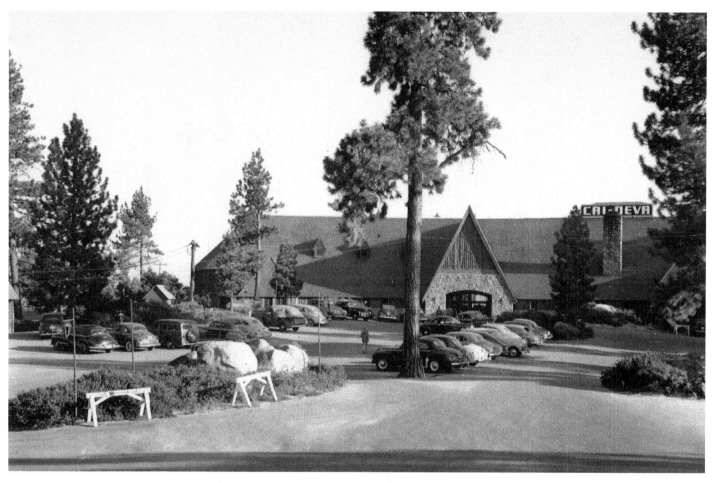

The Cal-Neva as she was when ol' Blue Eyes first fell in love with her. Sinatra bought the casino in 1960, installed a helicopter pad on the roof, and operated a guest list that included John F. Kennedy, Dean Martin, and Marilyn Monroe. When friend and mafioso Sam Giancana paid a visit, however, the state revoked his gaming license.

A tranquil day of sailboating during the height of the cold war. The Kennedy family used Lake Tahoe, and the Cal-Neva especially, as a Western retreat during this period.

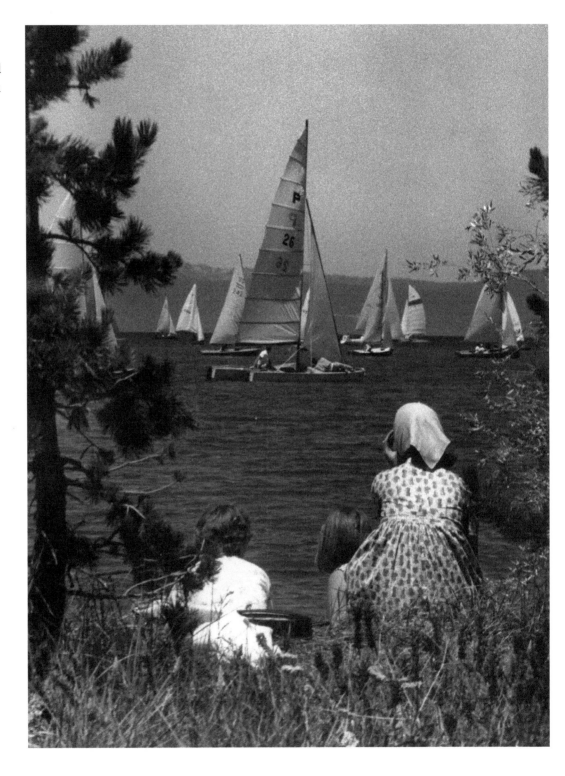

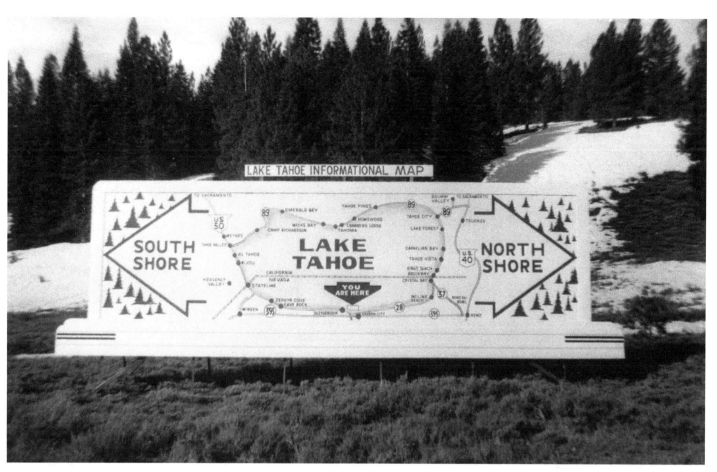

Lake Tahoe informational map. By the 1950s, the lake was ringed with resort communities and permanent residences.

Notes on the Photographs

These notes, listed by page number, attempt to include all aspects known of the photographs. Each of the photographs is identified by the page number, a title or description, photographer and collection, archive, and call or box number when applicable. Although every attempt was made to collect all data, in some cases complete data may have been unavailable due to the age and condition of some of the photographs and records.

69 **BROCKWAY HOTEL**
University of Nevada
UNRS-P2004-19-1

70 **POMIN'S LODGE**
University of Nevada
UNRS-P2003-15-31
N. E. Johnson

71 **TAHOE TAVERN 1920s**
University of Nevada
UNRS-P2272

72 **HANS HANSEN**
University of Nevada
UNRS-P1997-62-25

73 **NEWHALL PIER**
University of Nevada
UNRS-P1997-62-17

74 **DRUM ESTATE IN WINTER**
University of Nevada
UNRS-P1997-62-31

75 **RUBICON LODGE BEACH**
University of Nevada
UNRS-P1997-62-27

76 **TAHOE MERCANTILE COMPANY**
University of Nevada
UNRS-P1997-62-42

77 **SNOW-COVERED TAHOE TAVERN**
University of Nevada
UNRS-P1997-01-68

78 **CAVE ROCK TUNNEL**
University of Nevada
UNRS-P1989-11-15

79 **COOLING OFF AT BROCKWAY POOL**
University of Nevada
UNRS-P1993-05-344

80 **SUNSET AT CHONOKIS GIRLS CAMP**
University of Nevada
UNRS-P1993-05-426

81 **CAMPFIRE COOKERY AT CHONOKIS**
University of Nevada
UNRS-P1993-05-2010

82 **CHONOKIS GIRLS ON SNOWY CARSON PASS**
University of Nevada
UNRS-P1993-05-1018

83 **BAY VIEW RESORT**
University of Nevada
UNRS-P1994-03-15

84 **EVAPORATION PAN**
University of Nevada
UNRS-P2004-18-25

85 **CASINO DE PARIS**
University of Nevada
UNRS-P1992-01-7439

86 **MCKINNEY'S LODGE 1920s**
University of Nevada
UNRS-P1994-03-17

87 **CAL-NEVA ENTRANCE**
University of Nevada
UNRS-P1992-03-93

88 **CAL-NEVA LODGE**
University of Nevada
UNRS-P2007-04-31

89 **THUNDERBIRD MOTORBOAT**
University of Nevada
UNRS-P1997-58-314

90 **CAL-NEVA GAMBLERS**
University of Nevada
UNRS-P1992-03-98a

91 **THE CAL-NEVA BAR**
University of Nevada
UNRS-P1992-03-88

92 **THE CAL-NEVA FIRE**
University of Nevada
UNRS-P2004-18-120

93 **THUNDERBIRD LODGE**
University of Nevada
UNRS-P1997-58-299

94 **GEORGE WHITTELL IN SPEEDBOAT**
University of Nevada
UNRS-P1997-58-235

95 **MINGO**
University of Nevada
UNRS-P1997-58-57

96 **JOHANSSON DOG TEAM**
University of Nevada
UNRS-P2007-04-26

97 **BIRD'S-EYE VIEW**
University of Nevada
UNRS-P1997-01-71

98 **SKYLAND HOMEMAKERS CLUB**
University of Nevada
UNRS-P2000-06-1374

99 **INCLINE VILLAGE SUNBATHERS**
University of Nevada
UNRS-P1992-01-3380

100 **TAHOE CITY**
University of Nevada
UNRS-P1992-01-7330

101 **EMERALD BAY CAMP GUESTS**
University of Nevada
UNRS-P1993-03-1891

102 **GLOBIN'S AL TAHOE RESORT**
University of Nevada
UNRS-P1992-01-7419

103 **THE NEVADA CLUB**
University of Nevada
UNRS-P2007-04-23

104 **TA-NEVA-HO DINING**
University of Nevada
UNRS-P2007-04-15

105 **TAHOE INN**
University of Nevada
UNRS-P2007-04-27

106 **WASHOE INDIAN BOYS**
University of Nevada
UNRS-P1984-22-25

108 **STATE LINE COUNTRY CLUB**
University of Nevada
UNRS-P2007-07-4

109 **TAHOE TAVERN**
University of Nevada
UNRS-P2007-04-16

110 **TAHOE BILTMORE**
University of Nevada
UNRS-P1995-24-53

111 **TAHOE CITY 1940s**
University of Nevada
UNRS-P1992-01-7325

112 **TA-NEVA-HO CASINO**
University of Nevada
UNRS-P1992-01-3310

Printed in the USA
CPSIA information can be obtained
at www.ICGtesting.com
JSHW072025140824
68134JS00042B/3781

9 781683 368465